Unequal Crime Decline

Unequal Crime Decline

Theorizing Race,
Urban Inequality,
and Criminal Violence

Karen F. Parker

NEW YORK UNIVERSITY PRESS

New York and London

NEW YORK UNIVERSITY PRESS
New York and London
www.nyupress.org

© 2008 by New York University
All rights reserved

Library of Congress Cataloging-in-Publication Data
Parker, Karen F.
Unequal crime decline : theorizing race, urban inequality,
and criminal violence / Karen F. Parker.
p. cm.
Includes bibliographical references and index.
ISBN-13: 978-0-8147-6725-2 (cl : alk. paper)
ISBN-10: 0-8147-6725-7 (cl : alk. paper)
1. Crime—Sociological aspects—United States. 2. Crime and race—United States.
3. Criminal statistics—United States. 4. Urban violence—United States.
5. Social indicators—United States. 6. Violent crimes—United States.
7. United States—Social conditions. 8. United States—Economic conditions. I. Title.
HV6789.P39   2008
364.2'560973—dc22   2008012216

To Sammy, my Dad

* * *

To Sam and Aidan, my Sons

Contents

Preface

I began this book when my research on racially disaggregated homicide was moving toward incorporating change models. Over the last few years I had published articles addressing the link between racial stratification and urban violence. Much of this work dealt with ways to integrate labor market characteristics with criminological theories when examining race-specific homicide rates, investigating the link between racial competition and intra- and interracial homicide rates, and exploring the relationship between specific structural characteristics, such as concentrated disadvantage, and racial variations in urban violence. Although I was examining in my work various aspects of the link between race, urban inequality, and violence, it was all based on cross-section designs. In the early 2000s, when research on the crime drop was dominating the literature, I realized that the link between racial stratification and urban violence would be informed by this debate. My first attempt to incorporate change occurred in 2002, when I received funds from the National Institute of Justice (NIJ) to examine the link between economic restructuring and disaggregated homicide rates in 1980 and 1990. Then, in 2004, I published a paper examining the influence of changes in labor market and economic characteristics on black and white homicide rates in U.S. cities from 1980 to 1990. From this process I learned two important things. First, examining the influence of concentrated disadvantage on race-specific homicide rates did not capture the larger labor market characteristics in U.S. cities. The constructs of concentrated disadvantage and labor market structures, albeit related, were tapping two different aspects of the local urban economy. And while concentrated disadvantage was receiving a good bit of attention in the scholarly literature on violence, the nature of labor markets was not. Thus I realized that more research was needed on the changes in specific labor markets that were displacing workers in the urban context, contributing to the spatial concentration of disadvantage and rates of violence.

The second matter that surfaced was that change models were able to pick up on something quite different from the cross-section designs that dominate the literature. In light of the crime drop of the 1990s, incorporating change or a dynamic view was essential in my work, particularly since my research interests centered around changes in labor demand (such as deindustrialization) and the emergence of a "new economy" based on racial variation in the urban homicide rate. So when a publisher contacted me about writing a book, I knew it was time to finally merge two important areas of research—the relationship between racial inequality and urban violence, and the crime drop. This book, then, is my effort to investigate the relationship between race, urban inequality, and violence during times of dramatic change in both the urban economy and rates of city-level violence. It details how homicide rates have changed during the crime drop in U.S. cities but also documents trends before the crime drop. Key to the book is showing the differential patterns in homicide rates for race- and gender-specific groups over three decades and how the local urban economy is critical to understanding the unevenness in the homicide trends over time.

I extend my thanks to those who commented on individual chapters— Graham Ousey of the College of William and Mary, Don Tomaskovic-Devey of the University of Massachusetts-Amherst, Ron Akers of the University of Florida, and Patricia McCall of North Carolina State University—and others who were supportive of this project along the way. I have the deepest gratitude for Patty McCall, a good friend and collaborator, who spent a considerable amount of time and effort in generating a set of algorithms that was used to adjust the homicide counts for missing data. I also thank Robert Flewelling for his assistance with the adjustment procedure. I am grateful to all who helped shape this book— even before it was a book—by collaborating with me on various papers and projects. In addition to Patty McCall, I think particularly of Scott Maggard and John MacDonald. I appreciate the University of Florida for sabbatical time that allowed me to focus on this book, and also my colleagues at the University of Delaware for their support. I thank my parents who shared their vacation home with me and my children while I worked on this book during the summer months. My mom, who was already a good grandmother, turned out to be a good researcher, too, as she spent many hours carefully checking calculations by hand and pouring over stacks of spread sheets containing supplemental homicide counts. I especially thank the most important people in my life—Aaron, my spouse, and my sons, Sam and Aidan, for their patience and love. I thank my editor, Ilene Kalish, at New York University (NYU) Press, and her assistants, for making this process an enjoyable one. Ilene was supportive of this project from the beginning, but her support continued to the very end, as she gave me the time I needed to complete the project. I also thank the anonymous NYU reviewers who provided feedback on earlier drafts of the book. To all of you I will always be grateful.

1

Introduction

The study of urban violence has taken an interesting turn. After the turbulent 1980s, when reports of violence, drugs, and economic recession ran daily in major newspapers and media outlets, the crime drop of the 1990s in U.S. cities baffled academicians and the public alike. To our surprise, the lethal 1980s was followed by safer 1990s. Researchers rushed to understand what could cause this dramatic rise and fall in homicide trends over time. Conservation crime control policies, such as rapid incarceration rates and greater police presence, receding drug markets, and changes in gun policies were some of the possible explanations quickly gaining attention.

Few scholars have looked locally into urban areas for answers. A considerable shift has occurred in the urban economy since the 1970s, as the industrial and economic core of cities was largely transformed. Emerging as the "new economy," the latest economic transition to occur in urban areas has again changed the nature of work for most urban residents, many of whom were dislocated from earlier restructuring. Scholars have paid careful attention to the impact of deindustrialization on urban residents in the 1980s, including, to name only a few among notable others, Anderson's (1999) *Code of the Street* and Maher's (1997) *Sexed Work*. But few scholars have documented the larger economic shifts since the 1970s, which includes deindustrialization and the emerging new economy of the late 1990s on group relations, including crime trends.

It is these broader changes in the urban landscape over the last three decades that is of interest in this book. The role the local economy plays on the dramatic rise and fall in urban violence over time, though full of complexity, is one subject I examine. This is a sensible investigation, even a practical one, given the enormous body of literature linking economic conditions to crime. The motivation behind this book is not to repeat the unemployment-crime connection but rather to move the discussion forward. In fact, three fundamental facets of the urban landscape are noticeably lacking in attention, and it is my hope to bring them to light in this book.

The Uneven Nature of Urban Violence

Race and gender disparities in violence have been well documented in the criminological literature and official statistics for some time. According to the 2002 Bureau of Justice Statistics, African Americans were seven times more likely than whites to commit murder. Homicide is the leading cause of death among young African Americans, and we know that approximately 85% of violent encounters involves victims and offenders of the same race (e.g., black-on-black and white-on-white crime). Males represent the majority of homicide victims and comprise nearly 90% of offenders.[1] When race and gender are mutually considered, differences become even more pronounced. In 1986 the homicide rate for African American males was about six times higher than white males, and the African American female rate was approximately four times that of white females (Fingerhut and Kleinman 1989). Despite mounting descriptive statistics on the Bureau of Justice Web site or studies on the crime drop that disaggregates by multiple categories, including age, gun ownership, and race, little systematic effort was made to assess whether race and gender disparities in violence persist into the 1990s as the nation experienced the most remarkable crime decline in its history. Instead, during the 1990s, much of the homicide literature either directed its attention toward explaining the drop in total homicides or exploring the structural conditions that influence white and black homicide rates differently. These two areas of research have both grown considerably in terms of scholarly output and attention, but rarely have the two issues been merged together to address the disparate nature of the crime drop. The current literature, then, has largely failed to address whether the crime drop meant that the racial gap was increasing or narrowing (the recent exception is LaFree, O'Brien, and Baumer 2006) and what structural factors could be driving it.

The Local Economy

The economic changes that occurred in urban cities since the 1970s are many. Evidence of growing poverty concentration, joblessness, and distressed conditions in urban neighborhoods throughout American cities has been well documented. Many of these conditions have been linked to shifts in local labor markets, as big industry moved to the suburbs or overseas in pursuit of cheap labor. With any major shift in the local economy, the nature of work must also change. For instance, the Bureau of Labor Statistics suggests that between 1998 and 2006 almost all work (over 95%) created in the U.S. was based in the service industries (Hesse-Biber and Carter 2004). Changes, like these, in the economic climate filtrate into community life. Some residents will benefit from growth in the service sector, but others will not. Furthermore, Wilson warns that industrial changes occurring since the 1970s were unlike those in earlier decades. He claims that urban residents are less invested in the economic and social institutions of the area (Wilson 1987, 1991). Investments in the community are important, because they bring residents stability in times of economic downturn and change. Since the 1970s urban residents have been vulnerable to industrial and geographic changes in the local economy that have contributed to the growing concentration of poverty and joblessness, greatly impacting relations within and between groups. The changing nature of the urban economy has implications for the economic opportunities of various race and ethnic groups in urban cities. Yet these important changes, particularly how the characteristics of the local economy differentially impact the life chances of race- and gender-specific groups, has had no place in the discussion of the crime drop.

Changing Population Composition

The demographic makeup of cities has also changed considerably and, with it, the nature of group relations. Clearly U.S. cities are among the most race and ethnically diverse in the world. Looking back in time, the U.S. population more than tripled in a century (76 million in 1900, 281 million in 2000). In fact, a handful of states accounted for more than a third (38 percent) of the population growth in the twentieth century (i.e.,

California, Florida, Texas, and New York). To no surprise, these states are considered as "gateways" for immigration (Logan, Alba, and Zhang 2002; Clark and Blue 2004). In recent times urban areas have only become more diversified racially and ethnically. Whites no longer comprise the majority in some American cities (Clark and Blue 2004). Rather, Blacks and Latinos represent a large proportion in the city populace, as whites gradually move to the suburbs (Massey and Denton 1988). Hispanic (of any race) and Asian populations more than doubled in cities from 1980 to 2000 alone. Today, as researchers increase their attention toward immigration and adapt their studies to take a multiethnic approach, we learn of the unique experiences and history of Hispanics and Asians, experiences that differ from the black experience (Massey and Fong 1990; Fong and Shibuya 2005; Logan, Alba, and Zhang 2002). The labor market experiences of these groups are rooted in their own historic and political background. Yet shifts in the compositions of urban areas and population trends have received little attention in the crime-drop debate.

Here lies the impetus for this book. Essentially the changes in the demographic and economic climate of American cities have profound implications for the way we understand urban violence, including the crime drop. My goal, then, is to offer a coherent and comprehensive look at the relationship between race, urban inequality, and violence that is sensitive to these three important facets of American cities. Although my arguments emerge from the broader framework of race and urban violence, my focus is an area where this link has yet to be explored: the crime drop. After examining the ways that homicide trends differ by race and gender-specific groups over time, I offer some avenues to incorporate literature on race and the local economy into the study of the crime drop. And although criminological theories play a critical role in the study of urban violence, the link between theory and the crime-drop debate remains blurred. Apparently we are undecided about whether criminological theories are relevant to the decline in crime. In fact, there is little to no application of criminological theories—theoretical principles, concepts derived, or links proposed—to the steady decline in urban violence in the 1990s. As I attempt to link race, urban inequality, and violence, theoretical and empirical issues in the study of race and urban crime surface, leading me to consider the role of criminological theory in the crime-drop debate. Overall, the book has three main goals:

1. To illustrate how violence has changed significantly from 1980 to 2000 in urban areas, including the well-documented crime drop

of the 1990s, with attention toward how trends differ by race and gender-specific groups;

2. To assess existing structural theories of urban crime in terms of their ability to explain existing racial disparities in urban violence, particularly the dynamic or changing nature of urban violence over time; and

3. To theoretically explore the rise and fall in urban violence by offering linkages between race, urban inequality, and violence that are sensitive to the race- and gender-stratified nature of the local economy and the increasingly diversified composition of urban areas.

Throughout the book I take advantage of various literatures to address and at times integrate these themes. I build on stratification literature where the polarized nature of labor markets has been given considerable attention. The perspectives I review place race concretely in the structure of the economy, impacting the location and opportunity of race and ethnic groups in the labor force. Much like the stratification literature, criminological theories are pivotal to this book. I incorporate criminological theories that explore the structural characteristics which promote urban violence and contribute to the breakdown of social control within geographic areas. I draw also from feminist literature on labor markets and crime at various stages throughout the book. Although each perspective is valuable in its own right, I integrate these ideas when possible to offer a comprehensive look at the disparate nature of, and level of change in, urban violence over time. This pursuit of integration requires a macrostructural approach.

The Approach

The approach taken in the book is a structural one, that is, the book does not examine individual or situational characteristics in violence. Individual perspectives tend to focus on the personality of offenders, often neglecting differences in opportunity structures and the presence of structural factors associated with race, gender, and ethnicity. Instead, this book stresses the importance of examining how race and gender are embedded in the opportunity structures of urban areas, contributing to the spatial concentration of disadvantage for distinct groups and, as a result, producing conditions that lead to disparities in urban violence.

In many ways the approach is similar to Sampson and Wilson's (1995) chapter on racial inequality and urban crime. As a result of the publication of their work, the study of race, urban inequality, and crime has come a long way. We know more about the spatial dimensions in, and structural conditions associated with, urban crime. We also know how certain theoretical arguments fare, such as social disorganization and urban disadvantage, when applied to race-specific crime rates. For example, we now know that Wilson's idea concerning concentrated disadvantage (or the coupling of concentrated poverty with racial isolation) is relevant to white and black homicide rates. This book is similar in that it incorporates a mixture of ideas from sociology, economics, and criminology. By doing so, the broader macro-structural forces that contribute to crime trends for distinct groups take center stage.

Yet taking a structural approach brings its own set of challenges. For example, how does one conceptualize race and gender divisions that serve the basis of inequality in our society, yet still capture the long-standing inequality and symbolic meaning driving the differential treatment of these groups by others. When researching the word "race" for this book, for instance, I was amazed to find that scholars disagreed entirely on the meaning of the term (Alba 1992; Fredrickson 2002; Loury 2002). Race is a complicated concept, of course, but until now I had not fully appreciated the complexity of the term. Although we tend to define "race" as either "biological" or "social," the task of defining the term is far more intricate than a simple dichotomy suggests. In practical terms we categorize groups as whites, blacks, Hispanics, and Asians, yet theoretically we do not fully consider how these diverse groups are collectively "racialized" (Cornell and Hartman 2004). By the end of my search, like others, I found the biological versus social dichotomy unproductive and outdated, and the current efforts to measure race and ethnicity did little to reflect the diversity of the populations in which these words would apply.[2] Far more meaning is given to racial classifications, in that these words activate beliefs and attitudes, assumptions about individuals, and also affect access to resources (e.g., jobs, education, health care) and positions of wealth, power, and income. Thus "race" creates boundaries—spatially and interpersonally—and has enduring consequences. And the salience of race only grows in importance over time. Evidence can easily be found of this claim, such as the effort the census undertakes to provide new and different ways to measure race over time or the recent changes made by the federal government to categories groups by race and ethnicity (Hirschman, Richard, and Farley 2000). Within these efforts lies an important point: the way we conceptualize race and ethnicity changes over time. Recall how Italians and Eastern European Jews were seen as racial groups in the late nineteth and early twentieth centuries (National Research Council 2004) or how "Mexican" was included as a racial classification in the 1930 census bureau data collection effort, only to be discontinued after protests by the Mexican American community because of the stigmatizing effect it had (Cortes 1980; Hirschman, Richard, and Farley 2000). My point is that racial statuses change over time, as do the ways that we think and talk about them. Therefore our definitions must also change, as they are linked to the larger structural context. In this book, then, race is based on social and ascribed characteristics that have significant meaning for both the observer and the observed, and are informed by the larger economic and political climate.

In much of the literature, gender is as much about what we do as who we are. Just as "black" was an identity that revealed a sense of pride and power in the 1960s, empowerment is an attribute associated with gender, often reflecting something a person has or does not have. In this way, gender, much like race, demarks a process that is both interpersonal and social structural. Gender is used in this book to highlight the socially constructed differences between males and females rather than any biological differences that may be implied by the demarcation of "sex." For me, gender serves as a basis to identify and characterize where inequalities tend to form. Because our definitions of race and gender shift with the social, economic, and political times, these terms cannot be viewed separately from these institutions. In other words, gender, like race, is embedded in societal institutions, influencing ones access to resources, opportunities, and the ability to make decisions.

Changes in societal institutions, like the economy, can create barriers that exacerbate inequalities between groups; such institutions may also foster an environment in which inequalities are reduced. A prime example is racial discrimination. The idea that a wide range of racial disparities exists in economic and social realms is rarely in doubt. In fact, when drawing from a number of theories or previous studies, many researchers freely acknowledge that discrimination plays a role in our society. An African American female is fired because the employer feels uncomfortable working with her. A Hispanic male is passed up for a promotion because his employer feels he is not suitable for managerial positions. These acts of discrimination are recognized by scholars and the public alike. The issue, then, is how to capture discrimination in the aggregate, even those acts that are not based on stereotypes, emotions, or prejudices, such as the case with statistical discrimination (Baumle and Fossett 2005). Like other researchers, this challenge led me to turn to the existing literature for guidance. After a systematic review of studies that incorporated measures of racial inequality in the study of violence, I found numerous inconsistencies and a lack of theoretical clarity of the role inequality plays in the study of urban violence. In fact, the inconsistencies were so widespread that I felt it important to document them in this book (see chapter 3). Overall, there are challenges to overcome in the study of race, urban violence, and the crime drop that require us to broaden (not narrow) our definitions.

In short, a number of structural facets—both historic and contemporary—link race and gender to societal institutions. In this book I draw from various literatures that inform this notion and then apply these ideas in areas where they have not yet reached, namely, the current debate about the crime drop. What results is a book that deals with how inequalities, such as the stratified nature of labor markets and racial discrimination in housing, are produced and what form they take when contributing to the change in urban violence over time. Simply put, the book offers a look into this larger dynamic process that links race, urban inequality, and crime.

The Method

To examine trends, I cover major decade-to-decade changes in structural features of American cities in the period from 1980 to 2003. These trends are sometimes shown through maps, figures, or tables containing raw data, percentages, or change scores. Although the question of how to delimit labor markets and crime geographically may never be answered to anyone's satisfaction, the unit of analysis is any America city with a population base of 100,000 or more residents. The choice of U.S. cities is made purposely (see a full description in chapter 5). Census data are used to capture the structural characteristics of cities, and efforts are made to conceptualize the local economy and to incorporate indicators that tap major industrial and economic shifts in U.S. cities. To be precise, various charts and tables present data from decennial time periods and information reported by the Bureau of Labor Statistics (BLS).

In terms of displaying the changes in violence over time, researchers interested in crime trends are limited to two data sources for crime statistics: the Uniform Crime Report (UCR) and the National Crime Victimization Survey (NCVS). The strengths and weaknesses associated with these data sources have been well documented. In this book I use the UCR because it provides uninterrupted crime series data on offenders for U.S. cities. Specifically I draw from the Supplemental Homicide Files (SHF) because of the level of detail they provide on the characteristics of homicide victims and offenders. On the other hand, to overcome the problem of missing data, adjustments are made to the supplemental homicide data that make up the trends presented in this book. Missing data on the race of offenders is a widely known issue in the supplemental homicide files, and ignoring the issue of missing data was not an option (Messner, Raffalovich, and McMillan 2001; Williams and Flewelling 1987). Computations of all measures are outlined in the Technical Appendix, and all measures are based on original data.

Summary of Chapters and Key Findings

In this book I explore the structural characteristics of American cities that are influential to understanding the crime drop, particularly the way race and gender intersects with the local economy when contributing to the fluctuations in violence over time. Although undoubtedly a number of important factors are not explored here, I am particularly interested in incorporating dimensions of the new economy, as well as the old, into the study of the rise and fall in urban homicide rates. I argue that specific shifts in the U.S. economy, and, more directly, the embeddedness of race and gender in the urban economy, are plausible explanations for the crime drop. I build on existing literatures in stratification, economics, and criminology to fill this gap in the literature, and thus offer a dynamic view of race, urban inequality, and violence. Theoretical linkages are offered and statistical evidence is provided that show how an integrated approach of race and urban inequality can address the racial differences in homicide trends associated with the crime drop.

In this way, the book does not examine individual or situational characteristics in violence, nor does it offer a purely neighborhood- or community-level analysis. Rather, the book stresses the importance of investigating how race and gender are embedded in the structure of urban areas and, as a result, produce neighborhood conditions that ultimately lead to fluctuations in racial disparities in urban violence. Just as labor markets and the economy shift over time, rates of crime and violence also change dramatically. To illustrate these changes, I examine the peaks and drops in the urban economy and violence over three decades.

Chapter 2 is devoted to the task of displaying crime trends. Using UCR statistics, I provide statistical information on homicide trends for large U.S. cities from 1980 to 2003. Academicians commonly use homicide rates when documenting the crime drop, because homicides are the most accurately measured and reported offense compared to other crimes. When looking at trends in total homicide rates from 1980 to 2003, the rise and fall in urban homicides are easily noticeable. Although the rate of homicides rose in the late 1980s, starting in 1991 homicide rates began their steady decline until 2000, dropping approximately 46% over this period. A discussion of the leading explanations for the crime drop follows, including the rise in incarceration rates, police presence, and changing drug markets. As I review these explanations, however, little empirical support is found for any one of them. In fact, a lack of data and measurement issues plague this literature and restrict many efforts to test these ideas definitively. In this chapter I propose that the uncertainty surrounding this literature is also owing to the fact that the crime drop of the 1990s was not "universal." No single explanation, in other words, is likely to gain support in the empirical literature without some acknowledgment that the crime drop did not occur in all areas and among all groups. I argue that the pursuit for potential causes should reflect these important distinctions, where all-embracing explanations will not suffice.

To illustrate that point, what follows in chapter 2 is a detailed examination of homicide rates by race and by race- and gender-specific groups (e.g., black males, white females, etc.) over time. These rates are based on annual adjusted supplemental homicide data. Often masked by research using total homicide rates are important differences in trends and patterns by groups. This issue is amplified in the case of homicide trends associated with the crime drop. For example, black homicide rates rose in the late 1980s and dropped in the 1990s. An examination of the trends in white homicide rates, however, reveals a steady decline since the 1980s. Moreover, white homicide rates peaked in 1980, whereas black homicide rates peaked in the early 1990s. In terms of the level of the crime drop in the 1990s, the decrease in white homicide rates was considerably less in magnitude when compared to black homicide rates—white homicide rates dropped by 17% and black homicide rates by 44 percent in urban areas. Since 2000, white and black homicide rates continue to follow difference patterns. White homicide rates continue to decline, as black homicide rates rise. Other notable differences are discussed in this chapter, particularly those involving race- and gender-specific groups. To compliment this discussion, various figures and tables display trends and summarize important changes over time.

The question then becomes how to understand the rise and fall in homicide rates while acknowledging the unique trends by groups. Current explanations of the crime drop tend to focus on legal and political factors like incarceration and the presence of police. At the same time, research that incorporates racial disparities in urban violence and victimization rates often neglect to consider the drop in violent crime. Nor has criminological theories played a role in the crime-drop debate to date. To fill this void, I assess, in chapter 3, key macro-level criminological theories and the current research on racially disaggregated homicide rates.

Chapter 3 begins with a review of the macro-level theories most commonly used in the study of race and urban violence: social disorganization, conflict, and anomie/relative deprivation. Undeniably these are widely used and respected approaches in the study of violence. As leading explanations of urban crime, recent studies have applied these theoretical approaches to disaggregated homicide rates. However, support is weak for these theories in many studies. After documenting some of the inconsistencies and mixed, if not weak, support across studies of race-specific homicide rates, I offer reasons why I believe these theories struggle when attempting to explain the racial disparities in violence. One reason is that the theories tend to incorporate single concepts, like poverty, but fail to consider other ecological characteristics that shape the economic experiences of urban residents, such as access to labor markets and racial discrimination. Moreover, empirical tests of the theories tend to use the same measures, such as income inequality or poverty, without considering the theoretical relevance of these measures to core concepts or the structural forces that may reproduce these conditions within the urban context. For example, poverty is probably one of the most common indicators used in the literature, regardless of whether scholars are drawing from social disorganization or deprivation theories. Thus researchers often do not articulate *why* poverty levels differ greatly among racial groups. The emphasis on this concept has lead Sampson (2002) to call it "the poverty paradigm." Studies of urban violence have also neglected to incorporate change—a requirement if we are to give these studies serious consideration in the current debate on the crime drop. As a result, finding explanations for the crime drop represents a challenge to scholars, and criminological theories have neglected this call. Filling this gap, I argue, requires a multidisciplinary approach to understanding the relationship between race, inequality, and urban violence.

Chapter 4 explores the various literatures on race-relations/stratification, the economy, and sociology in an effort to begin the process of filling the void. This chapter provides evidence of how race shapes the urban experience by illustrating the racial disparities in labor markets and housing, as well as the impact of economic shifts in occupations and labor markets on the opportunity structures of various groups over time. Four important facets of American cities are highlighted in this chapter: industrial restructuring, the nature of work, degrees of racial separation and competition, and changes in urban populations that have transitioned these areas into multiethnic places. These four aspects of U.S. cities are central themes in the remainder of the book. And although each dimension is important in its own right, they tend to be interrelated. For example, population shifts through Hispanic immigration and the influx of other groups into urban areas influence residential segregation patterns and increase the job opportunities available to groups in urban areas. I argue that these four features accentuate American cities and, as such, are essential to understanding the race and gender differences in homicide trends associated with the crime drop.

Chapter 5 illustrates the ways that these arguments can be integrated with criminological explanations to address the crime drop. Specifically, concepts associated with these four facets of American cities are offered and theoretical ideas are proposed to expand our understanding of urban homicide. I argue, for example, that shifts in labor markets, the removal of specific industries in urban areas over time, and changes in the political economy are key contributors to the conditions that promote race and gender disparities in urban violence. I also show how these conditions have changed dramatically over the years, more so than poverty levels, and thus they are relevant to understanding the crime drop specifically.

To illustrate these claims, statistical information on the race- and gender-specific nature of opportunity structures and homicide rates are provided. For instance, I document the change in labor markets and the removal of manufacturing industries for various groups from 1980 to 2000 in a sample of large cities. Figures and tables summarize important patterns and changes in key concepts over time. This chapter concludes with a detailed look at two American cities, Detroit and Dallas, cities that are ideal for making a central point, namely, that the connections between race, the economy, and urban violence can best be understood in the multiethnic context of American cities. These two cities differ greatly on a number of important dimensions, showing that the dependency on a single indicator, such as poverty, does little to advance the literature on the crime drop.

Chapter 6 concludes by re-accounting for the race and gender dimensionality of urban life, and outlining some central themes surrounding the study of race, urban inequality, and criminal violence. The changing nature of violence is one of the most important issues facing criminologists, but our understanding of the crime drop will not fully be realized without considering the group differences that make up these trends. This discussion is linked to other important issues, such as the growing diversity of American cities, the rise in incarceration, and the lack of public support for key policies.

2

The Difference Race and Gender Makes

A Detailed Look at Violent Crime and the Crime Drop

Crime rates fell sharply in U.S. cities in the 1990s, plummeting the homicide rate to its lowest point in thirty-five years. Addressing these changes is the central focus of this chapter, which provides statistical information on the trends in violent crime for urban areas since the 1980s. Highlighted are the trends and patterns in violence for the total population and for distinct groups over time (1980 to 2003, specifically). These rates are based on supplemental homicide reports and adjusted for missing data using a formula created for use in this book (see Technical Appendix). Leading explanations for the crime drop are reviewed and discussed in relation to the detailed trends shown here.

The Crime Drop

The crime drop is common knowledge among academicians and the public alike. Figure 2.1 presents time series data for total homicide rates from 1980 to 2003, which is often used by academicians when documenting the crime drop (Levitt 2004; Blumstein and Rosenfeld 1998; Blumstein and Wallman 2001; LaFree 1999). In other words, because homicides are the most accurately measured and reported offenses, this crime provides the best benchmark. Additionally, because homicide is the most serious crime, it is the most widely used offense in research. For these reasons, it provides

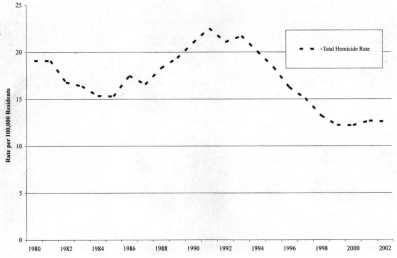

Figure 2.1. Total Homicide Rate per 100,000 Residents, 1980 to 2003

the most useful and accurate information about crime trends and, for my purposes, the greatest degree of comparability to existing studies.

The Trends

As shown in Figure 2.1, homicides averaged 19.09 per 100,000 population in 1980, and rates tended to fluctuate between 19.0 and 22.5 until 1991, when homicides peaked (22.52 per 100,000 population). A closer examination of this figure reveals that homicides dropped by 20% from 1980 to 1985, but then rose by 47 percent from 1985 to 1991. Starting in 1991, homicides steadily declined until 2000, reaching its lowest rate of 12.18 in 2000, or a drop of 46%. Since 2000, the rate of homicides has been stable over a three-year period. Visualized in this figure is the dramatic rise in homicides in the late 1980s, followed by a precipitous decline in the 1990s. The crime drop of the 1990s gained wide attention, and scholars searched for reasons for this unanticipated, yet welcomed, trend.

Contemporary Explanations for the Crime Drop

The drop in homicide rates occurred without warning, baffling many criminologists and policy makers (Blumstein, Rivara, and Rosenfeld 2000; LaFree 1999), and leading to an explosion of newspaper articles, TV reports, and other media accounts (see Levitt 2004). Scholarly atten-

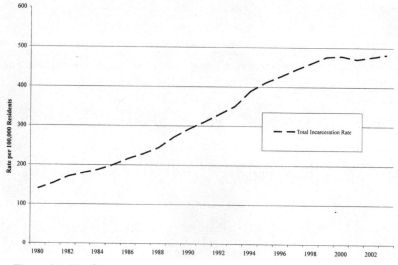

Figure 2.2. Total Incarceration Rate per 100,000 Residents, 1980 to 2003

tion soon followed with hypotheses proposed to explain this decline, including greater police presence, prison expansion, reduced handgun availability, tapering drug (specifically crack cocaine) markets, gains in the economy, and age shifts in the population (Blumstein and Wallman 2001; DiIulio 1995; Fox 1997). Although the list of possible explanations continues to grow, I briefly outline some of those that are receiving the greatest attention in the literature.

Rise in Imprisonment Rates. Any attempt to understand the changing nature of crime rates cannot occur without considering the political and legal context of the period. The enormous growth in "get tough on crime" policies that began in the 1970s is no exception. The expansion of the incarcerated population started in the mid-1970s, and by 2000 more than 2 million persons were incarcerated—four times the prison population of 1970. Figure 2.2 provides a look at total incarceration rates per 100,000 residents from 1980 to 2003, and documents the steady climb in the use of incarceration. The rise in incarceration rates corresponds closely with the decline in homicide rates shown in Figure 2.1, leading some researchers to link the two. For example, homicides were dropping from 1991 to 2001 in large cities, the very period when the Bureau of Justice Statistics reported that incarceration rates rose by 54.2% (or a rate change of 310 to 478 per 100,000 residents nationally). Olivares, Burton, and Cullen (1996) argue that this "get tough" movement had "a profound impact on the criminal justice system." The rise in incarceration is backed by structured sentencing, pressure to get violent and drug-related criminal offenders off the streets, and parole revocation, among other conservative trends in criminal justice policy (Kuziemko and Levitt 2003). Given the steady and prolonged trends in both rates of violence and incarcerations, it is not surprising that a number of scholars have linked incarceration to declining homicide trends during the 1990s (for notable examples, see Blumstein and Wallman 2001; and Levitt 2004).

Increase in Police Presence. One way to respond to rising crime rates is to hire more police officers. This political response is evident in annual figures of the Uniform Crime Reports. These reports tell of more police on the street, particularly in the 1990s when the FBI reports an extra fifty thousand to sixty thousand officers nationally (Levitt 2004). Efforts to link the police force to dampening crime rates are not new to the literature, particularly in light of studies offering strong empirical evidence that police reduced crime rates during the 1970s and 1980s (Marvell and Moody 1996). Figure 2.3 shows the level of change in police presence since the 1980s, marking the rise in the size of police forces across many large cities. In fact, this figure shows that the numbers grew by

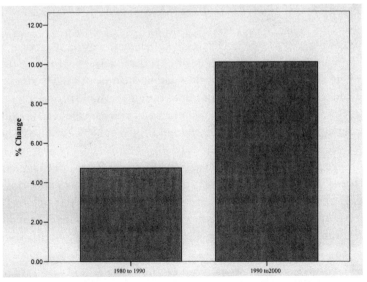

Figure 2.3. Percent Change in Police Force Size Rate
per 100,000 Residents, 1980 to 2000

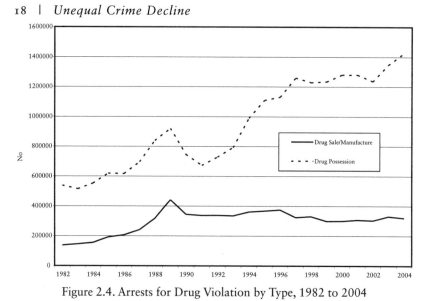

Figure 2.4. Arrests for Drug Violation by Type, 1982 to 2004

4% from 1980 to 1990, but the average growth was closer to 10% from 1990 to 2000. On average, the police force size was 236.1 per 100,000 city residents in 2000, up from 206.9 per 100,000 persons in 1980 in these cities. Based on these trends, scholars argue that increasing police presence is a likely predictor of the crime decline in the 1990s (Devine, Sheley, and Smith 1998; Levitt 2004; Marvell and Moody 1994, 1997).

Diminishing Drug Markets. The link between violence and illicit drug markets is another major contemporary explanation (Blumstein 1995). The growth in crack cocaine markets throughout the mid-1980s, peaking in the early 1990s, is related to homicide trends during this same period (Blumstein 1995; Ousey and Lee 2002). Drug markets contribute to violence (Goldstein 1985) and, as Goldstein et al. (1997) found, 25% of New York City's homicides were crack-related in 1988, a time of heightened city-level violence. Other studies have pointed to the importance of crack cocaine to patterns in violence (Blumstein and Rosenfeld 1998; Cook and Laub 1998; Cork 1999; Grogger and Willis 2000; Messner et al. 2005). Although research on drug-related crime is fraught with issues of how best to measure drug markets, one indicator of this type of drug activity is the number of police arrests for drug sales, specifically cocaine (Cohen, Felson, and Land 1980), particularly at the city level (Rosenfeld and Decker 1999; Ousey and Lee 2004). For example, Cork (1999), using city-level data, finds a significant direct relationship between juvenile arrests for crack and juvenile gun-related homicides. Figure 2.4 provides the annual FBI estimates for arrests of drug vio- lations involving sales/manufacturing and drug possession over time. The Uniform Crime Reports examined here show that drug arrests for sales/ manufacturing have exploded, growing two and a half times from 1982 to 2003 (from 137,900 to 330,600). The waning crack market in the 1990s or the increasing enforcement of drug sales in recent times, or both, has placed drug markets at the forefront of the debate on the crime drop.

The Improving Economy of the 1990s. Scholars have long pointed to the link between economic factors and crime (Chiricos 1987; Witt, Clarke, and Fielding 1999), so it is not surprising that the economic improve- ments of the 1990s has gained attention as a plausible explanation for the decline in crime. As shown in Figure 2.5, the unemployment rate rose during the recessions of the early 1980s and early 1990s, recovering after both periods. On the other hand, the unemployment rate steadily declined throughout the 1990s, where employment gains for males and females in the 1990s correspond to the crime drop of this period. In fact, the unemployment rate alone fell from 6.8 in 1991 to 4.8 in 2001 (or a drop of 30% in ten years). Other indicators of economic performance suggest better times for many Americans. Jorgenson (2001) estimated that the annual average rate of total-factor productivity growth increased in the 1990s, and much of the growth was the result of information tech- nology and an expanded service industry (see also Mann 2004; Oliner

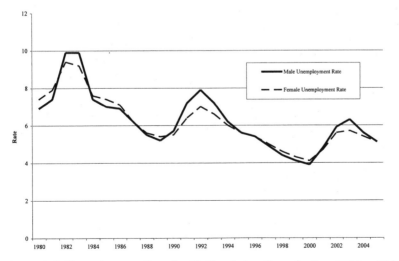

Figure 2.5. Unemployment Rate for Civilian Labor Force by Sex, 1980 to 2005

and Sichel 2000). Productivity growth is important, because it often translates into higher wages for the employed and better benefits for the unemployed (Appelbaum and Schetkat 1995). Thus the 1990s marked a time of sustained economic growth, and at the core of this growth was technology, productivity, and services. In fact, reflecting the significance of these technologies to improvements in the U.S. economy, the term "new economy" is now used by many economists (Eichengreen 2004).

Guns and Gun-Control Policies. A large percentage of homicides are gun-related, particularly during the 1980s and early 1990s (Cook and Laub 1998). Because the rate of violent crimes committed with firearms rose in the 1980s and 1990s and then subsequently dropped, some researchers have proposed that gun-control laws are a plausible explanation for this trend. Recently, however, scholars have downplayed the degree to which gun-control and concealed-weapons laws attributed to the decrease in crime (Levitt 2004). For example, Cook and Laub (2002) found that the percentage of total killings by young males remained stable during the period of the crime drop. Ludwig and Cook (2000) observed that the passage of the Brady Act had no influence on homicide trends.[1] And research evaluating gun buy-back programs and other gun-control policies determined that these programs also had little to do with the reduction in gun violence (Callahan, Rivera, and Koepsell 1994; Rosenfeld 1996; Reuter and Mouzos 2003; Kessler and Levitt 1999; Loftin et al. 1991; Raphael and Ludwig 2003). Even the highly publicized notion that concealed weapon laws are linked to lower violent crime has come under scrutiny (Lott and Mustard 1997);[2] in fact, more recent research has found that the decline in crime actually predates the passage of many concealed weapon laws (Duggan 2001), bringing serious doubts regarding any causal relationship between the two.

Although these explanations have been offered in the literature, unfortunately a lack of data and other measurement issues restrict definitive tests of many of these ideas. And even though a few studies have assessed one or more of these hypotheses (DeFina and Arvanites 2002; Grogger and Willis 2000; Gould, Weinberg, and Mustard 2002; Levitt 2001; Maltz 1998; Marvell and Moody 1994, 1996; Messner et al. 2005; Ousey and Lee 2002; Shepard and Blackley 2005), no one explanation is without criticism. In fact, empirical scrutiny has lead scholars to question whether some of these explanations even contributed to the crime drop, as illustrated by the research on the link between guns, gun-control policies, and violence. More specifically, although gun control was proposed as attributing to the crime drop early on, recent evidence suggests that guns and gun laws have little to do with the recent decline in crime.

Scholars continue to contemplate which factors may contribute to the decrease in crime, but definitive answers remain largely unknown. Recent in-depth examinations into this question have only clouded the issue. Given this, perhaps the pursuit for answers is hindered because the crime drop was not universal as claimed. Evidence has already surfaced that the crime drop is more complex than contemporary explanations have suggested. For example, the influence of guns and gun laws on the crime drop came under scrutiny when scholars found that homicides by young males remained stable over time (Cook and Laub 2002). If trends in violence differ across groups, such as by age, race, and gender, do our explanations for the decrease in crime not call for similar diversity? In this pursuit, I turn to time series data on homicide trends for race-specific groups.

Is There More to Know?

The fluctuations in total homicide rates from 1980 to 2003 are dramatic, particularly the well-documented decline in the 1990s. But, in reality, the trends are even more remarkable when disaggregated by race during this period. Figure 2.6 displays the time series data for total and race-specific homicide rates from 1980 to 2003. The magnitude of the black homicide rate is striking compared to the other two groups— the total and white homicide rates. In fact, two obvious differences are immediately apparent in the homicide trends displayed here. First, the homicide rate among blacks is much higher, with peaks and valleys more imposing than in the other two groups. Second, the change in white homicide rates over time is modest, to say the least, suggesting stability rather than variability when compared to others. For example, the white homicide rate has changed little over time, fluctuating between 5.9 (highest rate, 1980) to 4.1 (lowest rate, 2003) over a twenty-four-year period. Most notable in the white homicide rate is the lack of a peak around 1991 and little to no change in offending rates throughout the 1990s, unlike the other groups. A closer investigation of these data reveal some of the more subtle differences between these rates.

Black Homicide Trends. We see, in Figure 2.6, that the black homicide rate was 25.8 in 1980, compared to a total homicide rate of 19.0 per 100,000 city residents. Although the number of black homicides fluctuated between 25.7 and 21.7 in the period from 1980 to 1985, the rate dropped by 16% during this time. This drop is similar to the rate drop of 20% in total homicides. Between 1980 and 1991 black homicides ranged from 25.70 to 25.26 with the exception of a large dip in 1987 (19.43 per 100,000 population). In the 1990s, however, the crime drop in black homicide rates was considerable in magnitude, marking a 45% drop. Subsequently, however, black homicide rates increased during the 2000s (e.g., ranging approximately from 14.4 to 16.5 per 100,000 population).

White Homicide Trends. White homicide rates have changed since 1980, but modestly compared to black homicide rates. In fact, the decline has been slow and steady since the 1980s. White homicide rates peaked in 1980, reaching a rate of 5.89 per 100,000 white residents, whereas, in comparison, the total homicide rate peaked in the early 1990s. From 1980 to 1985 white homicide rates dropped 6.8% (5.89 to 5.49, respectively) and then dropped again, by 4.5%, in the late 1980s, only to continue to descend throughout the 1990s and into 2000 by another 17%. This decrease was far less in magnitude when compared to total and black homicide rates. Overall, white homicides averaged 5 per 100,000 white residents throughout the 1980s and into the 1990s. In 1998 white homicide rates dropped below 5 per 100,000 white residents for the first time, and since then the rates have

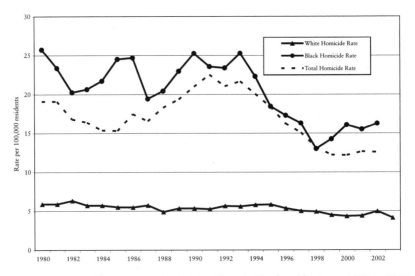

Figure 2.6. Homicide Rate per 100,000 Residents in Total and by Race, 1980 to 2003

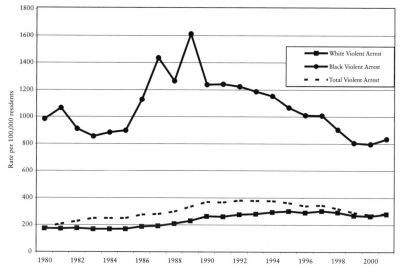

Figure 2.7. Violent Arrest Rate per 100,000 Residents by Race, 1980 to 2001

averaged from 4.0 to 4.5. Thus, unlike the considerable fluctuations in rates for the other two groups, the time series data indicate a steady decline in white homicide rates over the twenty-four-year period.

What about Other Offenses?

A comparison of arrest data with the homicide data discussed above is useful for various reasons. First it offers a different view of the crime trends in the U.S. Second, arrest data for violent offenses, a measure that combines arrests for murder, rape, robbery, and aggravated assault, are commonly used indicators of criminal activity in the literature (see LaFree, O'Brien, and Baumer 2006) and, unlike the homicide trends, include other violent offenses. Thus, unlike the homicide data, this measure captures overall trends in violence. Finally, arrest indicators are useful because these data can encapsulate police or social-control efforts which also fluctuate over time. That said, trends in arrest data involving violence should correspond with the homicide figures when considering the crime drop.

Figure 2.7 provides time-series data on violent arrest rates for the total population and for race-specific groups from 1980 to 2001. Overall, we can observe similar patterns to the homicide data provided in the earlier figures. In terms of the crime drop in the 1990s, the arrest data also show that the reduction in crime was more dramatic for blacks (36%) and for the total population (25%) than for whites. The most notable difference is the modest increase of 3.24% from 1991 to 2000 in white arrest rates. Essentially the similarity in the trends across these data sources suggests that the crime drop was not unique to homicide. The same general pattern appears for rates of violent arrests as for homicide offences, with the exception of the slight increase in the rates of violent arrests among whites. It is important to note that the arrest data support the claim that disparities exist between racial groups, although these disparities tend to narrow over time, particularly around the 1990s.

The Difference Gender Makes

The group differences in homicide trends call into question claims of the "universality of the crime drop" (see Levitt 2004, 167). Moreover, these figures reveal that the use of total homicide rates may be masking important information about the nature of the crime drop over time. This point becomes more evident when time series data on race- and gender-specific homicide rates are examined, although female homicide offending at the macro level has not received much attention until recently.

In fact, a prevalent concern among scholars is that research is often conducted without including the female offender (Chesney-Lind 1989; Daly and Chesney-Lind 1988), even though females account for about 22% of all arrests and 11% of murder arrests (Greenfeld and Snell 1999). The tendency in much of the criminological literature is to examine females as victims (rather than as offenders), offering qualitative or anecdotal accounts and proposing situational explanations at the individual level (see Acoca 1998; Bloom et al. 2003; Kaker, Friedmann, and Peck 2002; Koons-Witt and Schram 2003). Though rare in the academic research, when gender does take center stage, its influence is quite consistent and strong. Gender remains an important dimension in criminal behavior and, more specifically, it may play a key to understanding the crime decline if we take the time to consider it. One illustration comes to mind. Recent studies have highlighted the participation of young males in crack markets, and because these markets have receded in recent years, researchers suggest that declining drug markets are a predictor of the crime drop (Cook and Laub 1998; Cork 1999). Although drug markets have been advanced as an explanation for the drop in crime, far less has been said about the role gender plays (i.e., young males), even though scholars have long

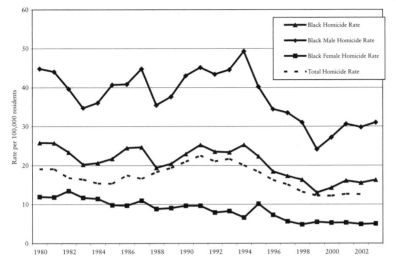

Figure 2.8. Black Homicide Rate per 100,000 Residents by Gender, 1980 to 2003

acknowledged the link between gender, participation in drug markets, and crime (Maher 1997; Fagan 1992). Underlining many explanations of crime are the ways in which gender structures one's activities and life chances; thus its applicability to the crime drop is equally plausible.

Black Homicide Rates by Gender. Figure 2.8 presents time-series data on black homicide rates by gender for the period from 1980 to 2003. For comparison, trends for the total homicide rate are provided in the background. Looking at the 1980 to 1991 period, black male homicides dropped 9% from 1980 to 1985, and then rose 11% to peak at 45.2 per 100,000 black male residents in 1991. On the other hand, black female homicides dropped by 18% from 1980 to 1985, only to drop another 2% in the late 1980s. In terms of the crime drop of the 1990s, black male homicides dropped 40% (from 45.2 in 1991 to 27.2 per 100,000 black male population in 2000), and black female homicides dropped 45% during this same period (from 9.63 to 5.26 per 100,000 population). Since 2000, black male homicides have increased, whereas black female homicide rates continue to decline.

White Homicide Rates by Gender. Figure 2.9 displays corresponding time-series data for white homicide rates by gender. Beginning in 1980, homicide rates for white males dropped by 10% (from 11.68 to 10.48

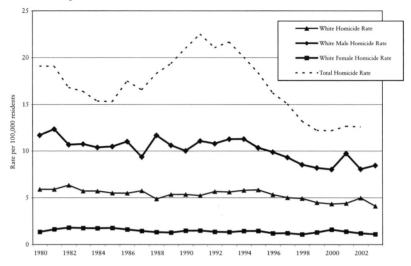

Figure 2.9. White Homicide Rate per 100,000 Residents by Gender, 1980 to 2003

per 100,000 white male residents) before ascending 5% to a rate of 11.01 per 100,000 in the late 1980s. On the other hand, white female homicides rose considerably until 1985 (a 31% increase) before dropping 16% in the late 1980s (from 1.77 to 1.49 per 100,000 white female population). And whereas white male homicide rates declined during the 1990s (from 11.08 to 8.04 per 100,000 population, or a 27% drop), homicide rates for white females rose by 6.7% (from 1.49 to 1.59 per 100,000 population). However, because the white female homicide rates are based on small estimates and contain larger zero counts, which are common to female violent offending data, the white female homicide trends should be interpreted with caution. Nonetheless, as these trends clearly show, gender makes a difference in criminal behavior (Belknap 2007; Daly and Chesney-Lind 1988; Messerschmidt 1986; Steffensmeier and Allan 1996; Steffensmeier and Haynie 2000) as well as in the nature of the crime drop.

Differences and Disparities

The figures presented in this chapter show the differential patterns in the crime drop, drawing into question recent efforts to explain the crime drop based on broad policies and general explanations. In an effort to summarize some of the key findings displayed in these figures, Table 2.1 provides summary information on the average homicide rates for select years and by groups, as well as data on the racial gap in homicide rates over time. If taken together, some interesting findings concerning the crime decline are apparent. First, the trends in black and total homicide rates are similar over time, but white homicide rates follow a different pattern. Specifically, whereas black and total homicide rates experienced a decline in the early 1980s followed by increases in the late 1980s, only to drop again in the 1990s, the decline in white homicide rates was more modest and steady over the twenty-four-year period. Second, gender makes a difference, in that trends for females differ from males when considering both within and between racial comparisons. For example, black male homicide rates rose in the late 1980s (by approximately 11%) as black female homicide dropped. The same trend is found among whites, whereby white male homicides also rose in the late 1980s (an increase of 5%) when white female homicide rates dropped by approximately 16% during this period. Another notable finding is that the percentage drop in black female homicide rates in the 1990s was larger than that of all the other groups.

Equally important is the degree to which the racial gap persists or narrows between groups. While this table provides evidence that

TABLE 2.1

Average Homicide Rates per 100,000 Persons for Select Years by Racial Groups

Group	1980	1985	1991	2000	% Change 1980– 1985	% Change 1985– 1991	% Change 1991– 2000
TOTAL & RACE-SPECIFIC GROUPS							
Total	19.09	15.30	22.52	12.18	-19.85	47.19	-45.9
Black	25.81	21.71	25.26	14.25	-15.89	16.35	-43.59
White	5.89	5.49	5.24	4.34	-6.79	-4.55	-17.18
RACE- AND GENDER-SPECIFIC GROUPS							
Black Male	44.85	40.72	45.17	27.19	-9.21	10.92	-39.8
Black Females	11.94	9.82	9.63	5.26	-17.76	-1.93	-45.38
White Males	11.68	10.48	11.01	8.04	-10.27	5.06	-26.98
White Females	1.35	1.77	1.49	1.59	31.11	-15.82	6.7
RACIAL DISPARITIES (RATIO OF BLACK TO WHITE)							
	6.03	5.62	6.22	3.88	-6.80	10.68	-37.62

Source: Adjusted SHF data.

racial disparities declined with the crime drop, some noticeable patterns emerge over time. When examining the racial disparities in homicide offending rates (via the ratio of black to white homicide rates) for select periods, disparities tend to shift with the homicide rates. In other words, during times when homicides rose for blacks between 1985 and 1991, the racial disparities in homicide offending also rose, an increase of 10.68%. On the other hand, as both black and white homicide rates were decreasing in the late 1990s, the racial disparities between these groups dropped considerably, by approximately 37%. This important dimension has only recently gained attention in the crime drop literature (see LaFree, O'Brien, and Baumer 2006). My findings support the claims made by LaFree et al. (2006), namely, that the racial gap has narrowed. However, by showing the distinct trends for racial groups in addition to the use of ratios, I find that the narrowing gap is largely attributed to the rapid decline in black homicide rates during the 1990s more so than that of whites. This finding alone adds considerable weight to the call for diversity in explanations applied to the crime drop debate.

Conclusion

Crime rates fell in the 1990s in many American cities. More specifically, violence peaked in 1980, subsequently dropping by 1985, only to rise again in the late 1980s. Since 1991, the rates have decreased sharply. The decline of the 1990s has received considerable attention by academicians and others, particularly because of the length of time involved (approximately ten years) and the sheer magnitude of the drop. Scholars have responded by proposing a number of explanations for this unanticipated trend.

Here I outline a number of leading explanations as to why crime declined in the 1990s. Many of these were made in response to time-series data on total homicide rates, although scholars have emphasized that trends differ considerably by age and other key demographic characteristics (Blumstein and Rosenfeld 1998; Cook and Laub 2002). While the list of plausible explanations has only grown over time, other explanations have lost ground as a result empirical scrutiny, such as gun laws. Nonetheless, our understanding of the crime decline has been limited by the absence of definitive tests and the lack of attention to these important differences in crime trends. In fact, most explanations to date are given without consideration of race and gender differences in crime trends, when we know that the duration and degree of the crime drop differs greatly for distinct groups. Indeed, white homicide rates have steadily declined since the 1980s whereas total and black homicide rates fluctuated greatly in the 1980s, with the decline starting around 1991. Unexplored is how contemporary explanations, such as those that focus on police force size or incarceration rates, hold up empirically to the modest (or lack of) change in white homicide during the 1990s. Furthermore, given that American cities are among the most racially and ethnically diverse in the world, the lack of attention to this reality when examining homicide trends at the city level is troubling.

Another concern is the neglect of criminology theories in the crime-drop debate. In fact, the discussion thus far has largely been void of criminology theory, focusing instead on political and legal aspects of the 1990s (e.g., incarceration rates, police presence, arrest rates, etc). Although no explanations can truly omit the political context of the time, criminological theories, particularly those that have endured the [empirical] test of time, may play an important role in explaining the crime drop.

Quite possibly, of course, criminological theories and contemporary explanations are interrelated; that is, the structural conditions deemed relevant to macro-level theories, such as unemployment, are likely contributors to crime and the criminal justice responses to it, such as police and incarceration. Scholars have noted, for example, the reciprocal relationship between crime rates and economic conditions of urban areas, and others have found that drug markets arise in response, at least partially, to limited job opportunities (Fagan 1992; Parker and Maggard 2005; Ousey and Lee 2004). Yet, despite the rather extensive body of research linking macro-level constructs to crime rates, criminological theories have yet to surface in discussions of the crime drop. In this vein, the next chapter explores the role of macro-level theories in addressing the racially disparate nature of homicide rates that make up these trends.

3

Structural Perspectives on Crime and Their Critics

As the crime drop continued through the 1990s and attention to this trend grew, scholars searched for answers in the political and legal changes of the time. The rise in incarceration, the expanding size of police departments, and declining unemployment rates were among the explanations pursued. Yet, as the crime drop was explored in more detail, the complexity of the decline became apparent, as did the recognition that these broad explanations were insufficient. Although political and legal factors are clearly relevant to the crime drop, more important is to link the decline in homicide rates with the diverse social and economic characteristics of U.S. cities. In this chapter I explore structural theories commonly used to explain homicide rates. How, in other words, might macro-structural theories advance our understanding of the crime drop? The focus is on three theories commonly called upon in urban homicide studies: social disorganization, anomie/relative deprivation, and conflict. Because these theories are not only leading explanations for urban violence but for race-specific homicide rates as well, I also assess the application of these theories to the study of racial disparities in homicide. The central question driving this discussion is this: how well will these theories advance our understanding of the differential nature of the crime drop?

Macro-Structural Theories: The Overview

Social Disorganization Theory

One of the most fundamental approaches to the study of violence emanates from the Chicago-school research of Shaw and McKay (1942). These scholars argue, in essence, that neighborhood dynamics lead to social disorganization in communities, which accounts for the variations in crime and delinquency. Here, "social disorganization" refers to the inability of a community structure to realize the common values of its residents and maintain effective social control (Bursik 1988). Key to Shaw and McKay's social disorganization model is the assumption that structural barriers impede development of the formal and informal ties that promote the ability of the community to solve common problems. These structural barriers result when urban areas experience changes in their social and economic structures, which builds on Burgess's (1967) "zone of transition." In this way, social and economic changes in a community shape structural conditions that impede group solidarity and contribute to the breakdown in social control.

Shaw and McKay identified three structural conditions—low economic status, ethnic heterogeneity, and residential mobility—as structural barriers that deteriorate a community's social organization. First, communities with low economic status lack adequate money and resources to generate the needed formal and informal controls necessary to reduce crime and delinquency. Second, racial and ethnic heterogeneity, which is often accompanied by fear and mistrust, impedes communication and patterns of interaction in a community. Third, residential mobility is said to disrupt a community's network of social relations by acting as a barrier to the development of extensive friendship networks, kinship bonds, and local social ties.

Although social disorganization theory became unpopular throughout much of the 1970s,[1] renewed interest in the theory has led to some important developments. First, researchers have extended the types of structural conditions in urban areas that impede social control, including population size, poverty, and family disruption (see Sampson 1986; Sampson and Groves 1989). Second, the mediating linkages between structural conditions, social control, and crime rates have been further articulated. While Shaw and McKay identified the capacity of the community to control group-level dynamics as a key mechanism linking community characteristics with crime rates, Sampson and Groves (1989) clarified the types of social networks in a community at both the informal and the formal levels, for example, friendship ties as well as participation in community organizations. They suggested that high rates of crime and delinquency will be experienced by those communities that are unable to (1) control teenage groups through collective social control, (2) form informal local friendship networks, and (3) organize local participation in formal and voluntary organizations (Sampson and Groves 1989).

More recently, Sampson, Raudenbush, and Earls (1997) conceptualized community ties somewhat differently to include the inability of community residents to collectively display trust and deal with problems (such as disorderly teens or drugs) by means of "collective efficacy," which has been found to largely mediate the relationship between structural disadvantage and crime (Sampson, Raudenbush, and Earls 1997; Sampson, Morenoff, and Earls 1999; Wells, Schafer, and Varano 2006).

Bursik and Grasmick (1993) offer another extension of the social disorganization model. Expanding Shaw and McKay's claims of the inability of communities to maintain social control, Bursik and Grasmick offer a "systemic model" linking community control to crime rates at three levels: private (friendships or households), parochial (organizational ties) and public (citywide efforts to regulate neighborhoods via police presence). Recent efforts to expand upon and extend social disorganization theory make the case for its relevance to the macro-level study of crime and add to a rather large body of literature supporting the social disorganization theory (Sampson 1985; Sampson 1987; Sampson and Groves 1989; Petee and Kowalski 1993; Smith and Jarjoura 1988; Smith and Brewer 1992).

Anomie/Relative Deprivation Theory

The idea that inequality contributes to crime has a long history in sociological theories, and Merton's theory of anomie is no exception. American culture places great emphasis on economic success, yet that culture's social structure impedes group access to this goal by placing barriers to the means that lead to success. The disjuncture between goals and legitimate means to achieving economic goals results in strain. Although Merton specified a number of ways that groups adapt to strain, some adaptations involve criminal innovation (Merton 1938). The term "relative deprivation," first elaborated by Merton (1947) and then Runciman (1966), exemplifies this process. Essentially economic success is the carrot dangling in front of individuals who have hopes and aspirations of achieving it, only to find the avenues blocked and considerably limited. The result is "intense pressure for deviation" (Merton 1968, 199), which was clearly voiced in Runciman's early writings:

A is relatively deprived of X when (1) he does not have X, (2) he sees some other person or persons, which may include himself at some previous or expected time, as having X (whether or not this is or will be in fact the case), (3) he wants X, and (4) he sees it as feasible that he should have X. . . . Given the presence of all four conditions, relative deprivation produces feelings of "envy and injustice." (Runciman 1966, 10)

In this treatment of relative deprivation, then, it is not only that the legitimate means are blocked and unrewarding, but also that the blocked means are accompanied by feelings of injustice and resentment. As persons become aware of their blocked economic resources and grow resentful, the potential for violence is present. Thus inequality suppresses the means to achieve material goals, contributing to feelings of frustration, which causes crime (Fowles and Merva 1996; Messner and Tardiff 1986).

Blau (1977) proposed that inequalities most closely associated with "ascriptive" status groups, such as race, are related to crime, whereas other inequalities may be seen as legitimate (i.e., those that are the result of hard work or education). In other words, feelings of deprivation that contribute to crime are often accompanied by racial inequality. Here theorists attempt to explain the response of certain racial groups to unfulfilled promises of justice and equity by suggesting that these racial groups are more likely to be deprived of economic resources. Where substantial economic differences between ethnic groups exist, members of disadvantaged groups are likely to feel antagonistic. These race and ethnic antagonisms comprise conflicts at all levels, including beliefs, behaviors, and institutions.

The most important feature of this argument is the clear implication that racial inequality is problematic primarily for certain racial groups. Minority groups are presumed to experience relative deprivation, which engenders frustration, and ultimately violence. This approach also postulates neighborhoods as the ecological arena where these social and economic comparisons are likely to be made. Residents living in the same neighborhood characterized with high levels of economic inequality will experience degrees of relative deprivation, and violence will thereby result. Drawing on how racial residential segregation could play a critical role in this process, Logan and Messner (1987, 511) claimed:

Residential segregation by race accordingly implies that opportunities for achievement are limited for certain groups, and it conflicts with basic American value commitments which encourage members of all groups to strive for socioeconomic success. Such a '"disjuncture" between structural arrangements and fundamental cultural values, Merton argued, tends to undermine the legitimacy of social norms and thereby promotes deviant behavior.

More recently, Messner and Rosenfeld (2001) built on the anomie/ strain tradition by further specifying the role of stratification in American society. Specifically they argue that the cultural emphasis on monetary success is further complicated by the dominance of the economy over other major institutions in society, such as family, school, and polity. The devaluation of education and family, compared to economic success, only further glorifies material gain, contributing to higher crime rates in the United States relative to our counterparts. Furthermore, the imbalance of power between other institutions and the economy only perpetuates inequality by weakening these institutions as a means for success.

Conflict Theory

If the two theories discussed above lead one to think that equal economic opportunity for all seems beyond our reach, might conflict theory offer a bit of optimism? By combining inequality with power, Marx described how capitalism produces an ever widening gap between the social classes. Although Marx wrote only sporadically about crime, other scholars have more systematically spelled out the connection between capitalism and crime. Capitalism, in the view of some scholars, is the root cause of crime (Greenberg 1993; Quinney 1974) by promoting ruthless competition and the exploitation of others in the pursuit of profits (Bonger 1969). And much like economic rulers pursue their own economic interests, they also work to ensure that government policies protect the advantageous position. As Reiman (1984) puts it, "the rich get richer and the poor get prison." Not only are laws shaped in such a way as to promote the interest of the powerful (Chambliss and Seidman 1980; Quinney 1975; Turk 1966), but criminal justice officials are not above breaking the law, using such avenues as a means of force and wrongful conviction (Holmes 2000; Chamlin 1989; Parker, MacDonald, and Jennings 2005).

Conflict criminologists tend to differ on how best to capture the economic deprivation that results from a capitalist state. Scholars differ, apparently, in terms of the importance of underlining the relative economic disparities by class or emphasizing the more observable conditions of this inequality, for example, poverty. Early works by Bonger (1969) and Quinney (1974) focused on the exploitation of the poor, suggesting that poverty-stricken groups may engage in more crime as a result of these inequalities. Other conflict theorists argue that economic stratification perpetuates conflicts, and thus it is the relative nature of the deprivation that affects crime rates. Whereas the conflict paradigm has drawn from both absolute (poverty) and relative (income inequality) forms of deprivation as sources of crime, others see similarities in these constructs, at least empirically (Bailey 1984; Peterson and Bailey 1988; Messner 1982). Despite conceptual differences, the solution to crime is a more equitable society. Both Bonger (1969) and Quinney (1980) note that the only end to this crisis is socialism. Even though the conflict approach offers an optimistic end, much of the literature tends to focus on the enduring consequences of economic inequality such as violent crime (Blau and Blau 1982; Hagan 1994: Hagan and Peterson 1995; Messner 1989; Short 1997; Williams and Flewelling 1988).

Two correctives to the conflict perspective have been found in the literature; one emphasizes the role of race and the other of gender in the larger economic stratification in our society. A feminist approach integrates gender, arguing that class location of women is related to the work they perform, even if unpaid (Phillips 1987). Scholars such as Messerschmidt (1988) clearly emphasize the importance of a broader social structure perspective that is inclusive of gender and capitalism. Specifically, Messerschmidt (1988) utilizes socialist feminist arguments to suggest that women are disadvantaged relative to men in both the paid and unpaid labor force because of the interaction between patriarchy and capitalism. The disadvantage associated with a patriarchal capitalist society significantly influences female involvement in criminal activity. But probably a more widely used explanation for female offending in recent decades is the economic marginalization hypothesis (see Box and Hale 1983; Chesney-Lind 1986; Datesman and Scarpetti 1980; Klein and Kress 1976; Heimer 2000; and Messerschmidt 1986). Both economic marginalization and socialist feminist perspectives work to provide a more comprehensive picture of the macro-level dynamics of gender, economics, and crime.

The conflict perspective has also been applied to address racial disparities in arrest rates, regardless of the level of involvement in criminal behavior. Drawing on the position that crime control is an instrument that powerful groups use to control groups that threaten their economic interests, Liska and Chamlin (1984) explain:

Conflict theory assumes that nonwhites have a substantially higher arrest rate than whites, because relative to whites, they are less able to resist arrest and because authorities share common stereotypes linking them to crime. (384)

But Hawkins has been vocal in his criticisms of conflict perspective, particularly its inability to account consistently for racial differences in crime and punishment. Hawkins's (1987) work suggests that the conflict perspective is inadequate when explaining the differential treatment of minorities in the criminal justice system. Furthermore, Hawkins argues that the conflict model fails to incorporate the racial characteristics of victims and offenders, the type of criminal behavior, and other considerations such as the response of the criminal justice system. After outlining the flaws in conflict theory and providing evidence of empirical inconsistencies in previous research, he offers a set of recommendations to resolve these theoretical limitations and research anomalies. Hawkins's claims, essentially, are that the use of conflict theory in criminology has been oversimplified, and, as a result, there is a general lack of theoretically driven works linking race to crime because of the larger dependency on conflict theory.

The significance of inequality, particularly economic inequality, is widely evident in each of these theories. Moreover, each approach acknowledges that structural barriers (such as poverty, lack of access to legitimate means, or economic inequality and capitalism) contribute to crime rates, and that these barriers are more pronounced among minority groups. It is important to note that nothing is stated within these theories that would suggest that any one demographic group is inherently more disposed to violence. Rather, the basic premise is that structural barriers, and cultural elements, in the geographical context leads to crime, possibly through undermining social organizations and community control, blocking opportunities, or creating power differentials and competition. It is these structural barriers that are linked to the disparities in crime rates, as they apply in larger degrees to some groups more than others. These theoretical claims have been widely used in the study of violence and, more recently, the study of race-specific rates of homicide. A review of this literature can aid in our efforts to understand the racial disparities in homicide rates and, as shown in chapter 2, the role criminological theories play when addressing the crime drop.

Theoretical Links to Race-Specific Homicide Rates

One book cannot do justice to the array of studies generated as a result of these three influential theories. In fact, it is beyond the scope of this chapter to review the empirical literature in detail. Doing so would only replicate the extensive work of other scholars (Blackwell 1990; Hsieh and Pugh 1993; Messner and Golden 1992; Patterson 1991; Pratt and Cullen 2005; Pridemore 2002). Chiricos (1987), for example, who reviewed sixty-three studies examining the relationship between unemployment and crime, has provided the most comprehensive look at this specific relationship to date. Hsieh and Pugh (1993) examined thirty-four studies on the effects of poverty and income inequality on crime rates, and Pratt and Cullen (2005), in the most recent effort to "make sense" of macro-level predictors of crime, have provided a meta-analysis of more than two hundred empirical studies. All these efforts focus on crime rates in the general population, for example, those relating to total homicide, violent crime, and property crime. Therefore, my focus here is on those studies that examine race-specific homicide rates under the rubrics of the three theories cited above, while making a few selective points along the way.

Table 3.1 provides a list of twenty-eight studies examining race-specific homicide rates.[2] As shown, the table divides studies by racial group, with those that examine black homicide rates listed first, followed by studies offering white homicide equations. While a handful of studies examine black homicide rates only, most studies offer both white and black homicide equations, and offer comparisons between models. When drawing conclusions, most researchers generally assess the similarities in magnitude and significance of parameter estimates included in homicide equations for blacks and whites. Few studies, that is, attempt to quantify or explicitly test the parameter differences using appropriate statistical techniques (with the exception of Ousey 1999 and Phillips 2002). Finally, all studies presented in the table utilize cross-sectional designs. In fact, few studies employ longitudinal examinations of race-specific homicide rates. Given the relevance of change to this book, these studies are examined separately at the end of this chapter.

A few points can be made regarding the studies presented in Table 3.1. First, the constructs offered across these studies overlap, with poverty, disadvantage, income inequality, and unemployment among the most commonly used. The tendency of these measures to dominant much of

TABLE 3.1

Summary Results of Economic Indicators Included in Race-Specific Homicide Rate Studies (N=28)

Source	Unit, N	Period	Findings- Key Economic Constructs		R^2
AFRICAN AMERICAN HOMICIDE					
Sampson (1985)	Cities, 55	1980	Poverty	+	
Sampson (1987)	Cities, 171	1980	Unemployment	0	.23
			% Families on Welfare	-	
			Per-Capita Income	0	
Messner & Golden (1992)	Cities, 154	1980	Resource Deprivation/Affluence	0	.228
Messner & Sampson (1991)	Cities, 153	1980	Male Employment	0	.28
			Per Capita Income	-	
			Public Assistance	-	
Parker & McCall (1997)	Cities, 168	1980	Economic Deprivation	+	.267
Parker & McCall (1999)	Cities, 196	1990	Resource Deprivation	+	.633
			Job Opportunity Index	nr	
			Job Access	-	
			Change in Employment	-	
Parker & Pruitt (2000a)	Cities, 175	1990	Resource Deprivation/Affluence	+	.360
			Job Accessibility	-	
Parker & Pruitt (2000b)	Cities, 89	1990	Poverty	+	.313
			40% plus Poverty Concentration	0	.284
Parker (2001)	Cities, 144	1990	Resource Deprivation/Segregation	+	.290
			Job Accessibility	-	
Parker & Johns (2002)	Cities, 144	1990	Disadvantage/Segregation	+	.504
			Job Accessibility	-	
Smith (1992)	Cities, 129	1980	Poverty	0	
			Unemployment	0	
			Income Intraracial Inequality	0	
Phillips (1997)	MSAs, 211	1990	Income Intraracial Inequality	+	.65
			Males Unemployed	+	
			Employed in Manufacturing	0	

Study	Unit, N	Year	Variable	Sign	
Phillips (2002)	MSAs, 129	1990	Poverty	nr	.425
			Income Intraracial Inequality	+	
Peterson & Krivo (1993)	Cities, 125	1980	Males Unemployed	+	.257
			Employed in Manufacturing	0	
			Income Intraracial Inequality	0	
Peterson & Krivo (1999)	Cities, 117	1980	Poverty	-	.361
			Professionals	0	
	Cities, 117	1990	Group Disadvantage	0	.375
			Concentrated Disadvantage	+	
			Group Disadvantage	+	.364
			Concentrated Disadvantage	+	
Krivo & Peterson (2000)	Cities, 124	1990	Concentrated Disadvantage	+	.383
Corzine & Huff-Corzine (1992)	MSAs, 149	1980	Concentrated Disadvantage	+	.384
			Percent Poor	0	
			Income Intraracial Inequality	+	
Harer & Steffensmeier (1992)	MSAs, 125	1980	Poverty	0	.0719
			Income Intraracial Inequality	0	
Wadsworth & Kubrin (2004)*	Cities, 154	1990	Deprivation	+	.198
			Income Intraracial Inequality	0	
			Job Access (ln)	0	
Kubrin & Wadsworth (2003)	C. Tracts, 114	1990	Disadvantage	+	.11
Hannon, Knapp & Defina (2005)	Cities, 134	1990	Poverty (Panel C only)	+	nr
Eitle et al. (2006)	MSAs, 166	2000	Disadvantage	+	nr
			Economic Segregation	+	
Ousey (1999)	Cities, 125	1990	Poverty	+	.281
			Unemployment	0	.267
			Income Intraracial Inequality	0	.266
			Deprivation	+	.277
Shihadeh & Ousey (1996)	Cities, 136	1980	Income Intraracial Inequality (M1)	0	.127
			Income Intraracial Inequality (M2)	0	.292
			Poverty	0	
			Welfare	0	
			Income Inequality (city-suburb)	0	

TABLE 3.1

Summary Results of Economic Indicators Included in Race-Specific Homicide Rate Studies (N=28) (continued)

Source	Unit, N	Period	Findings- Key Economic Constructs		R^2
AFRICAN AMERICAN HOMICIDE					
Lee & Ousey (2005)	Counties, 310	1990	Disadvantage	+	.319
Lee (2000)	Cities, 121	1990	Disadvantage	+	.154
			Poverty Concentration	+	.181
Shihadeh & Maume (1997)	Cities, 103	1990	Unemployment	0	.388
			Poverty	0	
			Job Access	-	
Shihadeh & Steffensmeier (1994)	Cities, 158	1980	Welfare	+	.75
			Income Intraracial Inequality	+	
Shihadeh & Flynn (1996)	Cities, 151	1990	Employment	0	.830
			Poverty	0	
WHITE HOMICIDE					
Sampson (1985)	Cities, 55	1980	Poverty	+	
			Unemployment	0	
Messner & Golden (1992)	Cities, 154	1980	Resource Deprivation/Affluence	+	.552
Messner & Sampson (1991)	Cities, 153	1980	Male Employment	0	.39
			Per Capita Income	0	
			Public Assistance	-	
Parker & McCall (1997)	Cities, 168	1980	Economic Deprivation	+	.465
Parker & McCall (1999)	Cities, 196	1990	Resource Deprivation	+	.553
			Job Opportunity Index	-	
			Job Access	nr	
			Change in Employment	0	
Parker & Pruitt (2000a)	Cities, 175	1990	Resource Deprivation/Affluence	+	.417
			Job Accessibility	+	
Parker & Pruitt (2000b)	Cities, 89	1990	Poverty	+	.570
			40% plus Poverty Concentration	+	.532
Parker (2001)	Cities, 144	1990	Resource Deprivation/Affluence	+	.514
			Job Accessibility	+	

Study	Year	Sample	Variable	Sign	Coefficient
Parker & Johns (2002)	1990	Cities, 144	Disadvantage/Segregation	0	.554
			Job Accessibility	0	
Smith (1992)	1980	Cities, 129	Poverty	+	
			Unemployment	0	
Phillips (2002)	1990	MSAs, 129	Income Intraracial Inequality	-	.544
			Poverty	+	
			Income Intraracial Inequality	0	
			Males Unemployed	0	
			Employed in Manufacturing	0	
Peterson & Krivo (1999)	1980	Cities, 117	Group Disadvantage	+	.298
			Concentrated Disadvantage	+	.304
	1990	Cities,117	Group Disadvantage	+	.343
			Concentrated Disadvantage	+	.376
Krivo & Peterson (2000)	1990	Cities, 124	Concentrated Disadvantage	+	.447
Harer & Steffensmeier (1992)	1980	MSAs, 125	Concentrated Disadvantage	+	.3593
			Poverty	+	
			Income Intraracial Inequality	+	
Hannon, Knapp & Defina (2005)	1990	Cities, 134	Poverty	+	nr
Eitle et al. (2006)	2000	MSAs, 166	Disadvantage	+	nr
			Economic Segregation	+	
Ousey (1999)	1990	Cities, 125	Poverty	+	.439
			Unemployment	+	.477
			Income Intraracial Inequality	+	.344
			Deprivation	+	.480
Shihadeh & Ousey (1996)	1980	Cities, 136	Income Intraracial Inequality	+	.397
Lee (2000)	1990	Cities, 121	Disadvantage	+	.321
			Poverty Concentration	+	.345

nr   Measure not included in model equation or not reported.

+   Positive, statistically significant coefficient.

-   Negative, statistically significant coefficient.

0   Non-statistically significant coefficient.

*   When studies separated intraracial from interracial homicide events, I include the intraracial homicide models only (e.g., Wadsworth & Kurbin (2004); Parker and McCall (1997, 1999). I used the black adult homicide models from Sampson (1987); Hannon et al. (2005) recommended 1 of 3 models (double-logged, panel C displayed here).

the homicide literature has been documented by others (see Pratt and Cullen 2005). Nonetheless, there are some differences in the ways these predictors have been used in race-specific analyses. First, unlike studies of total homicide rates, it is much more common for these indicators—poverty and income inequality, in particular—to be combined with other measures in studies of disaggregated homicide rates. Specifically, researchers are far more inclined to use composite indexes, typically generated through principal components analysis, to capture concentration effects and avoid the collinearity issues associated with including these measures separately in the same equation. The usefulness of factor or principal components analysis to deal with methodological issues has been well discussed in the existing literature (Land, McCall, and Cohen 1990; Messner and Golden 1992; Parker, McCall, and Land 1999). On the other hand, the use of composite measures means that you no longer can estimate the unique contribution of each construct in the race-specific homicide equation. This is particularly troubling, given my purpose here, which is to review previous findings concerning the influence of key measures. Nonetheless, it is quite clear that specific measures recur widely throughout the literature.

Second, although many of these indicators tend to be "strong" and "stable" in studies of total homicide rates (see Pratt and Cullen 2005; Hsieh and Pugh 1993), these words no longer describe how these indicators influence race-specific rates of homicide, particularly homicides involving blacks. For example, looking at Table 3.1, in studies examining African American homicide rates, the measure "poverty" was positive, statistically significant in four studies (Parker and Pruitt 2000b; Hannon, Knapp, and DeFina 2005; Ousey 1999; Sampson 1985) and non-statistically significant in eight studies (Harer and Steffensmeier 1992; Peterson and Krivo 1993; Phillips 2002; Shihadeh and Ousey 1996; Shihadeh and Flynn 1996; Shihadeh and Maume 1997; Smith 1992; Corzine and Huff-Corzine 1992). "Poverty concentration" was included only in two studies but with contradictory results. Parker and Pruitt (2000b) found that poverty concentration did not significantly influence black homicide rates, whereas Lee (2000) revealed a direct, statistically significant relationship. On the other hand, the relationship between poverty and white homicide rates was positive and statistically significant consistently in all seven studies (Parker and Pruitt 2000b; Phillips 2002; Harer and Steffensmeier 2002; Hannon, Knapp, and DeFina 2005; Ousey 1999; Sampson 1985; Smith 1992). Further, both studies including poverty concentration also found a positive impact on white homicide rates (Parker and Pruitt 2000b; Lee 2000).

The lack of comparability in black and white homicide rates produced by theoretical predictors has not gone unnoticed. Some scholars suggest that the variation in findings is theoretically confusing, if not outright contradictory to theoretical expectations. For example, when examining inequality within and between racial groups on homicide rates, Harer and Steffensmeier (1992) found that economic inequality predicts white homicide rates but was not predictive of black homicide rates, although they hypothesized that the effects of inequality would be higher for blacks based on Merton's anomie theory. When reflecting on this finding, they stated:

> That economic inequality has much smaller effects on black than white rates of violent crime is a powerful, albeit puzzling, finding. We speculate, drawing from Merton's anomie perspective, that this reflects a poorer articulation between structural (e.g., economic inequality) and cultural (e.g., egalitarian values, belief in upward mobility) contingencies among whites than among blacks. (1048)

Other studies exploring the link between income inequality and race-specific homicide rates had similar "puzzling" results. In the African American homicide equations, intra-racial income inequality produced a positive, statistically significant impact in five studies (Corzine and Huff-Corzine 1992; Phillips 1997; Phillips 2002; Shihadeh and Flynn 1996; Shihadeh and Steffensmeier 1994) and a non-statistically significant impact in six studies (Peterson and Krivo 1993; Harer and Steffensmeier 1992; Ousey 1999; Shihadeah and Ousey 1996; Smith 1992; Wadsworth and Kubrin 2004). In the white models, income inequality is non-significant in one study (Phillips 2002), negative in another (Smith 1992), but positive and statistically significant in three (Harer and Steffensmeier 1992; Shihadeah and Ousey 1996; Ousey 1999). On the other hand, the relationship between unemployment and the black homicide rate tends to be largely consistent across studies, yet findings are contradictory to theoretical expectations. For example, unemployment was not statistically significant in six studies on black homicide rates (Messner and Sampson 1991; Sampson 1985; Shihadeh and Maume 1997; Smith 1992; Ousey 1999; Shihadeh and Flynn 1996) but was positive in two (Phillips 1997, 2002). These inconsistencies not only cause concern but also raise important questions.

First, such findings question the assumption of racial invariance involving the influence of structural constructs on macro-level crime. Ousey (1999) dealt with this issue explicitly by providing a statistical test to compare correlates of black and white homicide rates across 125 cities in 1990. His findings confirmed what others had long suspected when comparing coefficients across race-specific homicide equations. To be precise, not only did Ousey find that many coefficients varied in magnitude and significance across the racial models but that measures, such as poverty, unemployment, and family structure, had a stronger impact on whites than blacks.

Second, studies tend to find that economic indicators produce findings consistently in white homicide models, but inconsistencies abound in black homicide equations. Moreover, economic indicators tend to be more powerful in predicting white than black homicide rates, often contradicting theoretical claims. For example, as illustrated above, the influence of poverty on black homicide rates varied widely across all studies, yet poverty had a positive, statistically significant influence on white homicide rates consistently across studies. Moreover, the amount of variance explained in white homicide models is far greater, sometimes two to three times higher, than that explained in black homicide rates. Let me point to a few studies as illustration. Messner and Golden's 1992 study reported the amount of variance explained as .228 in the black homicide model, compared to .552 in the white model.[3] Parker (2001) indicates an R^2 value of .290 versus .514 in black and white homicide models, respectively, and Harer and Steffensmeier (1992) report an R^2 value of .0719 in the black model but .359 in the white homicide model. Although some studies take note of this trend (Messner and Rosenfeld 2001; Wadsworth and Kubrin 2004; Parker and Pruitt 2000b; Hannon, Knapp, and DeFina 2005), few go as far to offer explanations. Of the handful of studies that report higher R^2 values in the black compared to the white equations (Parker and McCall 1999; Phillips 1997; Phillips 2002; Peterson and Krivo 1999), they offer multiple economic constructs that move beyond the more traditional ones in the literature, such as job accessibility and access to industrial sectors in urban areas, and integrate other theories outside criminology specifically. This expansion in theory and measurement appears beneficial to our efforts to understanding the link between race and urban violence.

In sum, there are some consistencies across studies, most noteworthy is the stability and strength that composite measures bring to race-specific homicide studies. The differences are far more numerous. In fact, the structural predictors most commonly used in the literature tend to produce the greatest inconsistencies. Moreover, the occurrence of inconsistencies is much more frequent in black homicide rather than white homicide equations. Finally, the inability for indicators to account for as much of the explained variance in black homicide equations as white homicide rates is concerning. It is troubling, in part, because some of the leading macro-level theories offer theoretical principles designed to address the higher arrests, if not offending, of blacks or minority groups or both. Phillips (1997) takes note of this tendency when concluding, "Contrary to several theoretical explanations, relative deprivation with respect to whites does not appear to be an important factor in explaining variation in black homicide" (548). If nothing more, this review of existing studies reveals that we know little about the relationship between race, structural conditions, and urban violence. In fact, there is much to uncover about which structural forces may be contributing to black homicide rates, relative to whites and other ethnic groups. Before taking on this important issue, some effort to explain why inconsistencies abound in much of the homicide literature is warranted.

Why So Many Inconsistencies?

To answer this question, we must look into the analytical strategies and statistical tools that researchers use. Without question, these studies differ greatly in time period, measurement, attention to missing data, handling of methodological issues such as partialing among regressors, outliers, and collinearity, and model specification. Parker, McCall, and Land (1999) and Land, McCall, and Cohen (1990) speculate that these methodological reasons are at the heart of the inconsistencies plaguing studies of homicide rates. More recently, researchers have utilized techniques, such as meta-analysis, to assess the contributions of macro-level predictors to crime rates. This technique is useful, because it provides information on the strength and stability of the mean effect size estimates for a set of measures, revealing which structural predictors are the strongest and the most stable (Pratt 2002; Pratt and Cullen 2005). However, neither identifying methodological flaws nor performing meta-analysis can disentangle the theoretical and conceptual underpinnings that are also contributing to the inconsistencies. In other words, as much as theory provides the footing and foundation for our work, the conceptual decisions we make can cause instability to occur in our models. Limitations of criminological theories have been previously noted (see Byrne and Sampson 1986; Hawkins 1987; Krivo and Peterson 2000; Parker and McCall 1999; Sampson and Wilson 1995; Sampson 2002). Here I speculate on the ways that these theories have been used in studies of race and urban violence that may cause some of these concerns. Specifically I offer five reasons that I deem critical, as they inform the course taken in the remainder of this book.

The Need for Meaningful Comparisons. As Sampson and Wilson (1995) note, the ability of researchers to make meaningful comparisons about the conditions that produce racial violence is significantly hindered by the fact that so few whites reside in areas of concentrated disadvantage when compared to blacks. It is difficult to establish which conditions produce rates of violence among distinct groups when comparable conditions do not exist. Harer and Steffensmeier (1992) acknowledge this as well, when finding that both overall and racial inequality were weakly associated with homicide rates. They write: "People assess how well, or badly, they are faring economically not by comparing themselves with the population as a whole, but with particular reference groups with whom they share some status attribute" (1036). Blacks are not likely to see whites as referents, or visa versa, if they live in geographic spaces that are so distant and dissimilar because of the segregated nature of urban neighborhoods. This reality presents a challenge to researchers when they try to compare the influence of structural predictors on white and black homicide rates across equations.

Some researchers have found ways to overcome this issue. One avenue is to compare race-specific crime rates when the levels of structural disadvantage faced by whites and blacks are comparable. In studies that pursue this path, researchers found that structural conditions, such as concentrated disadvantage and homeownership, have similar effects on white and black homicide rates, which supports the racial invariance thesis (Krivo and Peterson 2000; McNulty 2001). Although this strategy makes sense, it is in some ways an analysis of "outliers," as the majority of black neighborhoods have no white counterparts. Thus, by requiring the comparison, this research is unable to explain why such vast differences exist.

Another option is to directly model the black-white differentials in homicide rates (Sampson, Morenoff, and Raudenbush 2005; Phillips 2002). Phillips (2002) took this approach by applying the Oaxaca decomposition technique to determine whether the group differences in homicide rates result from differences in the *level* of structural conditions facing racial groups or from the different *effects* structural conditions have across groups. This technique further enabled Phillips to assess whether the differentials in racial and ethnic groups could be reduced if these groups were exposed to similar geographical circumstances. This research produced two important findings. First, Phillips found differences in both process and effects for a series of structural predictors on black, white, and Hispanic homicide rates. She found, in other words, that structural predictors of homicide differed by racial group and, further, that there was also great variability in the strength of the predictors, suggesting that differences in the process were also present. This finding supports the claims made by other scholars, but here Phillips was able to quantify these differences more explicitly. Second, Phillips revealed that the black-white differential or racial gap in homicide rates was largely a function of the dissimilarities these groups face in the ecological environment. Specifically, she concluded that almost half of the black-white homicide gap can be attributed to group differences in family structure and socioeconomic conditions.

The reality, then, is that blacks and whites reside in areas that are ecological dissimilar, particularly regarding the economic characteristics of their local area. And although some researchers have attempted to overcome this issue in their empirical studies, the remaining challenge is why the majority of whites and blacks do not share the same ecological environment. This issue requires researchers to explore the process, as well as the consequences, associated with such an existence. Currently research does not yet address "*why* black and white neighborhoods as a whole occupy such different places on the distribution of economic advantage and crime" (Sampson and Bean 2006, 12; emphasis in original).

Construct Dominance. As the review of previous studies reveals, researchers have the tendency to use the same predictors repeatedly. This construct dominance is likely because of data limitations, as many macro-level studies are dependent upon census data. But the tendency has a theoretical element as well, similar to what Sampson called the "poverty paradigm" (Sampson 2002, 216), namely, that criminologists have focused far too long on poverty as a central concept. This trend is clearly evident in systematic reviews of homicide research (Pratt and Cullen 2005, for example), where poverty and other economic indicators such as inequality and unemployment are commonly found. This trend has only grown in frequency after the publication of Wilson's seminal book, *The Truly Disadvantaged* (1987), of which the concentration of poverty was a central theme. Although poverty is undeniably linked to social disorganization, just as income inequality is to anomie and unemployment to conflict, these "outdated" (Sampson 2002) measures have a reoccurring role in the macro-level studies of violence.

Given the prominence of these constructs in the homicide literature, we assume they are relevant to changes in homicide as well, like the crime drop. In chapter 2 I offered recent improvements in the economy as one of the leading explanations for the crime drop, as some researchers have linked declining unemployment rates during the 1990s to lower crimes by youth (Freeman and Rodgers 1999; Gould, Weinberg, and Mustard 2002). However, many economists question the link between unemployment rates and the crime drop because unemployment rates tend to fluctuate significantly over time, showing short-term changes (ibid.). Whereas economists point to the cyclical nature of unemployment rates, criminologists/sociologists find further issues with unemployment rates, as this indicator tends to exclude those who fall outside the civilian labor force, such as people who are not actively seeking work, who face a spatial mismatch in terms of the location of jobs and their residency, or who have weak labor force attachments. Because of the exclusivity of this measure when capturing the disenfranchised worker and economists' reservations concerning the measure's ability to pick up long-term changes, unemployment is an unlikely determinant of the crime drop. Could other commonly used economic indicators hold a similar fate? That is, could poverty and income inequality also prove problematic when addressing the crime drop?

Table 3.2 provides the bivariate correlations between various race-specific economic indicators commonly used in the literature and homicide rates in large U.S. cities. Although the left side of the table reports the average level of economic deprivation from 1980 to 2000, the aim here is to show the degree of change in these constructs during times of rising and falling homicide rates using change scores.[4] During the 1980s, when homicide rates were increasing, economic deprivation among whites and blacks was also on the rise. For example, black poverty increased by an estimated 5% and within-race income inequality rose by approximately 9%, with black homicide rates increasing by approximately 12% during this same period. On the other hand, whites experienced rising poverty rates (6.5%) and within-

TABLE 3.2
*Average Scores, Percent Change, and Bivariate Correlations (r) Between
Economic Indicators and Homicide Rates During Times of Rising and
Falling Homicide Rates*

Group	1980	Mean 1990	2000	% Change 1980– 1990	r	% Change 1990– 2000	r
RACE-SPECIFIC ECONOMIC INDICATORS[a]							
Black:							
Poverty	26.3	27.6	25.1	4.94	.180*	-9.06	-.002
Income Inequality	.409	.445	.435	8.80	.098	-2.25	-.056
Joblessness	54.2	55.3	51.2	2.03	-.070	-7.41	-.068
White:							
Poverty	9.95	10.6	11.4	6.53	-.068	7.55	.008
Income Inequality	.352	.415	.396	17.90	-.092	-4.82	-.015
Joblessness	58.4	60.8	59.7	4.11	.105	-1.81	-.058
RACE-SPECIFIC HOMICIDE(S) RATES[b]							
Black				11.99		-43.59	
White				-0.63		-17.18	

a. U.S. Bureau of Census decennial data for 1980, 1990 and 2000; intercensal data not available for cities.
b. Adjusted SHF data; statistically significant bivariate correlation at < .05 (two-tailed test).

racial income inequality (approximately 18%), but their homicide rates changed little (0.63%). Much like unemployment, it is difficult to believe that a link exists between the patterns of change in these economic indicators and crime. Moreover, only one of the bivariate relationships reaches statistical significance. This trend continues when looking at the 1990s as the economy was improving, even though homicide rates were dropping. Here, again, none of the bivariate relationships is statistically significant, thereby suggesting that changes in these economic constructs do not correspond to the changes in homicide rates. Although these measures are prominent in the criminological literature, they do not capture the change in the local urban economy that may be driving trends in homicide.

Yet other constructs, largely ignored in much of the literature, may be tapping some important economic shifts. Drawing from Wilson's (1987) work, scholars have incorporated other economic indicators such as concentrated disadvantage, removal of manufacturing or low-skilled jobs from the inner city, and job-opportunity structures (for example,

Phillips 1997, 2002; Parker and McCall 1997, 1999; Wadsworth and Kubrin 2004; and Ousey 1999) and, more recently, "economic segregation" (Eitle, D'Alessio, and Stolzenberg 2006). It is worth noting that these constructs and composite measures tend to increase the stability in results and enhance the amount of the variance explained in black homicide rates. For example, in all race-specific homicide studies that include a deprivation or disadvantage index or both, a positive, statistically significant effect was found, with only two exceptions across the twenty-eight studies included in this chapter (e.g., Messner and Golden 1992; Parker and Johns 2002). The consistency and stability associated with composite measures are encouraging and suggest that efforts to explore different avenues to account for economic conditions, both theoretically and empirically, are promising.

Discrimination as a Theoretical Measure. One of the most pervasive aspects of American history is, unfortunately, discrimination. Although sociologists have a broad spectrum of definitions, Levin and Levin (1982) define "discrimination" in a way that embodies the "differential or unequal treatment of the members of some group or category on the basis of their group membership rather than on the basis of their individual qualities" (51). Some scholars have argued, however, that this definition does not acknowledge how deeply embedded discrimination is in our societal institutions, particularly regarding our economy. Offering an alternative explanation, Feagin and Eckberg (1980) defined discrimination as "practices and actions of dominant race-ethnic groups that have a differential and negative impact on subordinate race-ethnic groups" (9). Although definitions differ, scholars tend to agree that discrimination on the basis of race, color, sex, or national origin remains pervasive. This notion was of central concern to civil rights laws and most theoretical discussions of discrimination. For example, the passage of the 1964 Civil Rights Act made racial discrimination illegal in access to voting, schools, public accommodations, and employment in the United States. Nonetheless, minorities continue to bear the negative consequences of discrimination.

Given this social reality, I examine the ways that researchers have included aspects of discrimination in studies of race-specific homicide. Drawing from the same group of studies reviewed earlier, the results are displayed in Table 3.3. First, "racial inequality" has commonly been used in studies to denote the disparities between racial groups. This concept tends to include one or more ratio indicators that reflect black-white

TABLE 3.3
*Summary Results for Racial Inequality, Segregation
and Race-Specific Homicide Rates (N=19)*

	Racial Inequality		Racial Residential Segregation	
	African Americans	Whites	African Americans	Whites
Sampson (1985)	-	0	—	—
Messner & Golden (1992)	+	+	NR*	NR*
Parker & McCall (1997)	0	NR*	NR*	NR*
Parker & McCall (1999)	0	0	NR*	NR*
Parker & Pruitt (2000a)	0	0	NR*	NR*
Parker & Pruitt (2000b)	0	-	+	0
Parker (2001)	0	0	NR*	NR*
Parker & Johns (2002)	0	0	NR*	NR*
Phillips (1997)	0	—	+	—
Phillips (2002)	—	—	0	0
Peterson & Krivo (1993)	0	—	+	—
Peterson & Krivo (1999)	0	0	+	0
Krivo & Peterson (2000)	0	0	0	0
Hannon et al. (2205)	—	—	0	0
Ousey (1999)	—	—	0	-[a]
Lee (2000)	—	—	NR*	NR*
Lee & Ousey (2005)	0	—	0	—
Shihadeh & Steffensmeier (1994)	0	—	—	—
Shihadeh & Flynn (1996)	—	—	0[b]	—

* Racial Resedential Segregation was combined with other indicators in a composite measure; NR = not reported.
a. In Ousey's (1999) multiple model study, segregation has a positive effect in some models and a nonstatistically significant effect in others.
b. Shihadeh and Flynn (1996) also included P (black/white interaction) indicator of segregation, which produced a negative, statistically significant effect.

differences in income, unemployment, and education. Although "racial inequality" is commonly included in studies of disaggregated homicide rates, this measure rarely reaches statistical significance. For example, in nineteen studies examining African American and white homicide rates, an effect for "racial inequality" was offered some twenty-four times but was statistically significant in only two studies (see Messner and Golden 1992; and Sampson 1985). Beyond debating methodological issues and causes, we must question whether we are capturing the adverse treatment of race and ethnic groups in our empirical work.

Researchers are showing increasing awareness of racial residential segregation as a core condition in urban areas. In fact, some scholars suggest that racial discrimination in housing may be the best indicator of racial discrimination in American cities (Massey and Denton 1993; Ondrich, Ross, and Yinger 2000; Yinger 1995), arguing that racial residential segregation is the "structural linchpin" of racial relations in the United States (Pettigrew 1979; Bobo and Zubrinzsky 1996). When drawing from this literature, scholars have illustrated how racial segregation contributes to the geographic concentration of poverty for many groups (Wilson 1987; Massey and Denton 1993). In an effort to measure social isolation, many researchers use the "index of dissimilarity" that captures the distribution of white and black residents in census tracts. The index ranges from 0 to 100, where 0 indicates that blacks and whites are distributed evenly across tracts and 100 reflects tracts where whites and blacks are completely segregated. According to Massey and Denton (1993), an average index score in most urban cities was 60% in the 1980s, suggesting that 60% of blacks or whites would need to change their neighborhood residency in order to achieve a racially balanced residential environment. Other measures of segregation have been offered (Massey and Denton 1993), but the index of dissimilarity is by far the most common in the homicide literature.[5]

As shown in Table 3.3, measures of racial residential segregation are bound by economic disadvantages, which support theoretical claims of concentration effects (Wilson 1987) and the role racial residential segregation plays in the economic concentration of poverty among blacks (Massey, Gross, and Shibuya 1994). However, of those studies that offer an indicator of segregation separately from other constructs, some inconsistencies emerge. In the African American homicide models alone, for example, four studies report a positive, statistically significant relationship between racial segregation and black homicide rates (Parker and Pruitt 2000b; Phillips 1997; Peterson and Krivo 1993, 1999), and six studies indicate non-statistically significant effects (Phillips 2002; Krivo and Peterson 2000; Hannon, Knapp, and DeFina 2005; Ousey 1999; Lee and Ousey 2005; Shihadeh and Flynn 1996). The inconsistency, again, may be the result of how we apply the theoretical arguments. For instance, some scholars propose that the link between racial segregation and crime rates is mediated by economic disadvantage. Thus a significant direct effect is unlikely. Nonetheless, we must question whether or not we capture racial discrimination in our theories and if studies are truly able to measure (or control for) the influence of racial discrimination on urban violence. One recent study reports a relatively low correlation between indicators of racial inequality and racial residential segregation (see Eitle, D'Alessio, and Stolzenberg 2006), although both were offered as indicative of the same core concept—racial discrimination. Clearly the complexity of discrimination as a concept contributes to the challenges we face when finding ways to measure discrimination (National Research Council 2004). Despite the difficulty, researchers must be committed to moving beyond definition and measurement problems. Because of a lack of theoretical attention and inconsistencies in results, this hurdle remains to this day.

Lack of Theoretical Clarity. Distinct from the tendency to incorporate the same economic indicators in the homicide literature, discussed above, a related issue is the inclination to offer economic indicators (poverty, unemployment, and income inequality) in studies of crime without attention to theoretical detail. Where Tittle (1983) warned of a social class bias in criminological research some twenty-five years ago, Pratt and Cullen (2005) have provided explicit evidence of this inclination. In a sample of 214 macro-level studies, Pratt and Cullen were able to produce 153 effect size estimates for the influence of poverty on crime. Income inequality and unemployment were documented with similar frequency, where these scholars were able to reproduce 167 and 204 contributing effect size estimates for these measures, respectively, on crime rates in their sample of studies. Although these measures were commonly used across studies, the authors noted that it was difficult to establish which indicators corresponded to each macro-level theory; they stated: "many of the macro-level predictors of crime assessed in this study cut across multiple theories" (430). Later they provided an example of this point using unemployment, stating:

> Researchers have used measures of unemployment as proxies of guardianship (routine activities theory) and economic hardship (economic/resource deprivation), as an indicator of a breakdown in the viability of community control/socialization (social disorganization theory), and even as a precursor to frustration-induced anger (anomie/strain) theory). (430-431)

This quote illustrates the lack of theoretical specificity on the part of researchers when offering major constructs at the macro-level. Furthermore, this tendency becomes all the more complicated in the literature on race-specific homicide rates. Though race-specific measures of poverty are commonly offered in dissagregated homicide studies, few researchers consider what causes poverty nor do they attempt, more specifically, to address theoretically the vast racial disparities in poverty levels in urban settings.

It is quite possible that the structure-versus-culture debate, which dominated much of the violence literature throughout the 1970s and 1980s, slowed theoretical progress in this regard. Instead of more clearly testing structural theories by developing theoretical arguments and addressing conceptual issues, researchers were debating whether the determinants of violence were associated with structural characteristics or cultural predispositions. Today, scholars have clearly moved beyond this debate by suggesting an integrated framework, where subcultural value systems conducive to crime emerge in structurally disadvantaged communities (Brunson and Stewart 2006; Sampson and Bean 2006; Sampson and Wilson 1995; Horowitz 1983; Anderson 1999; Kubrin and Weitzer 2003). Another trend is assessing the mechanisms of informal social control or attenuated culture on community-level violence (Sampson, Raudenbush, and Earls 1997; Warner 2003; Sampson and Bean 2006; Sampson and Wilson 1995).

One must wonder if political concerns surrounding the study of "race and crime" have also impeded theoretical developments. As Sampson and Wilson (1995) stated:

> The discussion of race and crime is mired in an unproductive mix of controversy and silence. At the same time that articles on age and gender abound, criminologists are loath to speak openly on race and crime for fear of being misunderstood or labeled racist. (37)

If not political nuance, then certainly the complexity that the concept of "race" brings to the study of violence may have slowed the pace of progress (Alba 1992). Regardless of the reasons, the research is bound by a lack of theoretical clarity. Also, few researchers have attempted to move beyond the use of "outdated concepts" in their investigations of urban violence (see Sampson 2002) or fully explore the structural forces contributing to heightened poverty levels in inner cities, which divided racial groups geographically in urban communities.

Overlooking the Dynamic Processes. Fundamental to Chicago-style criminology is its attention to dynamic changes in urban neighborhoods and crime (Bursik 1988). In fact, the changing nature and level of spatial interdependency between neighborhoods is embedded in the social disorganization tradition (Sampson 2002; Morenoff, Sampson, and Rauden-bush 2001). Yet the element of change, once core to the theory, has been largely neglected in the existing research. In an effort to sway research-ers, Byrne and Sampson (1986) called for longitudinal analysis:

> By far the vast majority of ecological studies have examined the relative effects of structural characteristics on crime in cross-sectional analysis at one point in time. This is somewhat ironic given that classic ecological theory is concerned with the processes of change in urban areas. (17).

Some twenty years later, Sampson reiterated this troubling trend toward cross-section research when he said: "And almost no research has exam-ined *changes* in community-level processes" (216; emphasis in original). He went further to argue that the lack of research had caused a series of fundamental questions concerning our understanding of cities and com-munities.

Cross-sectional designs also largely dominate the macro-level research derived from anomie and conflict-based theories. In fact, one can find few examples of empirical research that examines changes in macro-level characteristics and crime rates over time (examples include Fowles and Merva 1996; Baller et al. 2001; Messner et al. 2005), and far fewer have assessed race-specific homicide rates (LaFree, Drass, and O'Day 1992; LaFree and Drass 1996; Messner, Raffalovich, and McMillan 2001). By far the greatest impediment to longitudinal analysis is data, although some researchers have overcome this issue to offer change models. Con-ducting national time-series analyses of the rates of white and black arrests, LaFree and colleagues found differences in the influence of eco-nomic indicators on white and black arrest rates over time (LaFree, Drass, and O'Day 1992; LaFree and Drass 1996). For example, based on their longitudinal analysis between 1957 and 1990, LaFree and Drass (1996) found that income inequality (as a measure of resource depriva-tion) has a positive impact on the changes in white and black arrest rates but that absolute economic well-being (their composite measure that combines median income and unemployment) did not significantly influ-ence homicide rates for either racial group.[6] Unlike LaFree and Drass (1996), Messner, Raffalovich, and McMillan (2001) found that unem-ployment and poverty were related to arrest rates among youth between 1967 and 1999. Although Messner and colleagues noted that the differ-ences in the results of the two studies could be due to measurement, they further stated: "Unfortunately, few clear theoretical guidelines in the literature can be relied on to govern the selection of specific measures of inequality" (605).[7]

It is no surprise, then, that macro-structural theories are easily brushed aside when the focus turns to the crime drop. In fact, theoretical ambiguity over measures and the failure to examine change over time in empirical studies has largely made criminological theories irrelevant to the crime drop, with few exceptions. After examining UCR crime trends, LaFree (1999) offered explanations for "the 1990s crime bust," including economic stress, political legitimacy, and family disorganization—all constructs commonly found in macrostructural theories. LaFree's work is one of the only examples of research on crime trends that incorporate theoretical perspectives. But he, too, acknowledges the precarious position of criminological theories when the question turns to the crime drop. He claims that researchers were "caught off guard" by the crime drop, largely because of the heavy reliance on cross-sectional designs in criminological literature.

Conclusion

The criminological theories of social disorganization, anomie, and conflict have a long and important role in the study of urban crime, and yet complications abound. As researchers apply these theories to disaggregated crime rates and search for answers for the crime drop, they will face challenges in their pursuits. One difficulty is that although criminological theories speak to the changes in urban areas as contributors to urban violence, few studies investigate change or offer longitudinal studies. Efforts to do so will require researchers to utilize methodological advances of recent years. Researches will also need to move beyond more commonly used concepts such as poverty if theories are to address the changes in crime rates over time. This chapter illustrated the tendency to define economic conditions in terms of poverty and unemployment at the same time that scholars neglect to consider other aspects of the local economy such as labor markets and industrial sectors. The predominance of some constructs over others has also been documented by others (see Pratt and Cullen 2005). If current concepts and measures commonly used in criminology to reflect structural characteristics of urban areas are producing inconsistencies and contradictory results, then we must expand our efforts theoretically and conceptually to locate other literatures that might better capture the ecological concentration of race and the economic dislocation of groups that may be driving the differential patterns in the crime violence.

For reasons outlined in this chapter, among others, a void or gap exists in our understanding of the crime drop and the relationship between race, inequality, and urban violence. There is little doubt that criminological theories are relevant to the study of urban violence, just as legal and policy changes are relevant to the crime-drop debate. What is unknown is the role criminological theories play in the study of the racially disparate nature of the crime drop and how specific economic and social conditions have converged with legal changes when influencing the crime trends of the last three decades. For example, changes in the economic climate of urban areas impact not only crime rates but also the ways in which the criminal justice system responds, such as expanding the size of the police force and its use of incarceration. Drug (crack cocaine) markets are also in response, at least partially, to limited economic prospects and rising unemployment and poverty rates (Fagan 1992). Since the presence of drug markets tends to drive away employers and legitimate, more desirable businesses in the inner city (Ford and Beveridge 2004), disenfranchised workers turn to crime as disadvantages rise. These and other examples show that the paths and linkages between structural characteristics, criminal justice policies, and crime are multiple and diverse. Exploring these paths and pursuing other concepts are critical to understanding the larger dynamic process of race, inequality, and criminal violence, and, more directly, the crime drop. Acknowledging the limitations of criminological theory, let us turn our attention to research in social stratification and economics.

4

Racial Stratification and the Local Urban Economy

The Civil Rights Act of 1964 was one of the greatest advancements in American history. As noted, racial discrimination regarding access to voting, schools, public accommodations, and employment in the United States was declared illegal. Organizations and workplaces were pressured to desegregate and, in adherence to one of the goals behind the Civil Rights Act, to integrate whites with blacks, males with females. Although racial and ethnic groups have made advances both politically and economically since the 1960s, neither legal change nor political pressure has altered the pace of workplace desegregation to where employment parity has become a reality. Almost four decades later, race and gender segregation persist in the workplace.

The link between race and employment has long occupied our historical record. Drawing from stratification literature, where the segregated nature of work has been given considerable attention, I examine three perspectives that place race within the structure of the economy, influencing the location, opportunity, and level of racial competition in labor markets: industrial restructuring and the concentration of disadvantage, the role of racial segregation, and racial threat/competition. It is not my intent here to provide a full description of each perspective—the originating authors and subsequent studies have done so quite well in various works. Rather, my goal is to call attention to central themes in the stratification literature that establish the structural roots of race in labor market opportunity structures in U.S. cities. In that pursuit, the spatial concentration of disadvantage and race/gender segregation in labor markets becomes lucid. The themes identified here are used later to establish the linkages between racial stratification and urban violence. But first let us examine the perspectives from which these themes are derived.

Industrial Restructuring and the Spatial Concentration of Disadvantage

Wilson (1987) claimed that the increase in economic marginalization of blacks in the inner city was largely owing to a set of spatial and industrial changes in the political economy. In *The Truly Disadvantaged*, he pointed to deindustrialization, coupled with suburbanization of middle-class African Americans, as central to the rise in poverty and social isolation among inner-city residents. Central to his arguments, Wilson illustrated the dramatic shift away from local manufacturing-based economies during the 1970s and 1980s, particularly in the Midwest and Northeast regions of the United States (Bound and Holzer 1993; Kasarda 1995). Advances made in technological industries contributed to this shift, as did the motivation to secure cheaper labor and the growing demand for service industries. The process of deindustrialization marked a change in the industrial mix of urban areas or, more specifically, how the share of jobs shifted from manufacturing to administrative and information services in many American cities (Kasarda 1995). Residents of these cities were adversely affected in a number of ways.

First, shifting manufacturing jobs into the suburbs or overseas (Harrison and Bluestone 1988; Kasarda 1989) and changing the industrial mix of local economies resulted in a spatial mismatch; that is, the number of low-skilled jobs in the inner city was reduced, and blacks, because of residential segregation, were unable to follow employers to the suburbs (Zax and Kain 1996). Further, the low wages associated with manufacturing work limited inner-city residents from seeking employment outside their neighborhoods and city boundaries (Holzer 1991). Thus, as central cities were transformed into service-based economies and centers for administration and information processing (Kasarda 1989; 1995), the number of potential employment opportunities available to low-skilled workers was reduced in these areas (Wilson, 1992). In the words of Packer and Wirt (1992), the requirements of the new economy created a "skills mismatch" between workers and the service jobs available to them, further disadvantaging blacks living in the inner city.

Second, preexisting segregation in labor markets because of discrimination in hiring meant that the ill effects of deindustrialization were predominantly felt among minorities and the poor. Indeed, scholars have linked the high rates of joblessness among black males to the transformation of the U.S. economy or industrial restructuring (Bound and Holzer 1993; Kasarda 1983; Katz and Murphy 1992; Jaynes and Williams 1989; Wilson 1987). And although the literature examining the influence of restructuring on women is small and inconclusive, some researchers found that women actually benefited from industrial restructuring since the shift increased the number of jobs in female-dominated service occupations (Jones and Rosenfeld 1989). However, others argue that black women lost job opportunities with the expansion of service-based industries (Browne 2000; Kletzer 1991). Like black males, black women were more likely to work in the manufacturing sector than white women (Bound and Dresser 1999: Glass, Tienda and Smith 1988), resulting in higher levels of dislocation for this group (see examples in Tienda, Smith, and Ortiz 1987). Tienda and colleagues (1987) found, moreover, that Latino and black women faced greater declines in jobs than Asian and white women, suggesting that the already high levels of economic marginalization among women was further concentrated among minorities (Browne 1997; Ihlanfeldt and Sjoquist 1989). Adding to the crippling effects of industrial restructuring on women, the disabling of welfare and the elimination of federal welfare entitlements, such as Aid to Families with Dependent Children (AFDC) to black women with children who were disproportionately represented (U.S. Department of Commerce 1993), only further guaranteed that African American women would be vulnerable to shifts in the local economies.

Deindustrialization also contributed to the ever increasing social isolation and racial segregation of African Americans in urban cities (see also Kasarda 1989, 1992; Kaufman 1986; Ricketts and Sawhill 1988). The concentration of poor in the most disadvantaged areas meant that inner-city residents were forced to take employment for wages barely large enough to provide for their families (Wilson 1992). Capturing the social transformation of urban areas, Wilson's term "concentration effects" reflects the continued deterioration of employment opportunities and job networks, the decline in schools, and the diminishing numbers of marriageable partners, thus contributing to higher levels of family dissolution, which only further aggravated the weak labor attachments and conventional role models for inner-city residents (Wilson 1987, 58). Thus workers facing industrial restructuring had detrimental consequences in the labor market and beyond, as this shift also had consequences for their communities and families (Anderson 1999; Wilson 1996).

Racial Residential Segregation

Although Wilson acknowledges that discrimination played a role in industrial restructuring, Massey and colleagues (Massey and Denton 1993; Massey, Gross, and Eggers 1991; Massey, Gross, and Shibuya 1994) make the connection explicitly. Agreeing with Wilson's claims that deindustrialization increased the spatial concentration of poverty among African Americans, Massey (1990) argues that racial residential segregation in U.S. society plays a much larger role in this process than previously demonstrated. In a series of seminal pieces, Massey documents the trends toward housing discrimination that contributed to widespread racial residential segregation in many urban cities. Although many Americans consider racial segregation a historical artifact associated with times prior to the Civil Rights movement, and many criminological theories dismiss discrimination as a core concept, the research by Massey and colleagues provides an eye-opening account of race relations in American cities.

Though Massey and Denton (1993) found support for Wilson's claims concerning the growing concentration of poverty, they argued that the primary cause of the rise in concentrated poverty among African Americans throughout the 1970s and 1980s was racial residential segregation. While eliminating out-migration of middle-class African Americans as a contributor, Massey and colleagues linked the rise in African American poverty rates to intra-racial residential segregation by class and high levels of African American/white residential segregation (Massey, Eggers, and Denton 1994). Whites' residential preferences for intra-racial residency has limited chances of racial integration while perpetuating the concentration of poverty disproportionately among African Americans as they face discrimination in the housing markets (Massey 1990; Massey and Eggers 1990; Massey, Gross, and Eggers 1991). No single work makes this point more clearly than Yinger's (1995) *Closed Doors, Opportunities Lost*. In his examination of housing discrimination against African Americans and Hispanics during the early 1990s, Yinger found discrimination at every point of the real estate process, from the very first call to a real estate agent to the point where the applicant is ultimately denied a mortgage. Documenting real estate steering to neighborhoods dominated by persons of the same race and the efforts of real estate agents to show only certain properties, he found that a black person had a 60%

probability of facing housing discrimination, which increased to 90% when the interested buyer visited up to three agents. Though discrimination was more pronounced among blacks than Hispanics, the significant levels of discrimination experienced by both groups was undeniable. In fact, scholars have extensively documented housing discrimination specifically against African Americans, as well as Hispanics, that shaped residential patterns (Massey and Denton 1993; Alba and Logan 1992; Farley et al. 1978). Such practices included, as described above by Yinger (1995), real estate agents steering racial groups to certain neighborhoods and unequal access to mortgage credit, but also exclusionary zoning that restricted racial groups to particular neighborhoods and neighbor hostility (Alba and Logan 1991; Massey and Denton 1993; Massey and Mullan 1984; Ross and Turner 2005; Yinger 1995).

Studies on segregation have found that white-black segregation levels are too high to be explained by economic differences alone, even when economic status is measured by education, income, or occupation (Farley 1977; Iceland and Wilkes 2006). As Massey and Denton (1993) stated, housing discrimination not only contributes to racial residential segregation but also binds minorities to other forms of disadvantage:

> We readily agree with Douglas, Pinkney, and others that racial discrimination is widespread and may even be institutionalized within larger sectors of American society, including the labor market, the educational system and the welfare bureaucracy. We argue, however, that this view of black subjugation is incomplete without understanding the special role that residential segregation plays in enabling all other forms of racial oppression. Residential segregation is the institutional apparatus that supports other racially discriminatory processes and binds them together into a coherent and uniquely effective system of racial subordination. (8)

The interaction between racial residential segregation and inequality created a concentration of poverty within the poorest African American neighborhoods—a spatial reality known to few others. African Americans experience higher levels of poverty than whites and few whites reside in areas of extreme disadvantage compared to African Americans (Wilson 1987; Sampson and Wilson 1995; Krivo and Peterson 2000). Furthermore, in their 1994 study, Massey, Eggers, and Denton found that the high levels of African American poverty also resulted from low wages and earnings among African American workers in manufacturing and the service industry. Thus the relationship between racial residential segregation and the concentration of poverty is both direct via discrimination of housing markets and indirect through local labor markets (Massey, Eggers, and Denton, 1994). Whether one views racial segregation patterns as a result of discrimination, particularly toward blacks as compared to Hispanics and Asians (Alba and Logan 1991; Massey and Fong 1990), or a result of the urban context where whites resist integration of local labor and housing markets (Farley and Frey 1994; Frey and Farley 1996; White, Fong, and Cai 2003), persisting patterns of black segregation from whites in U.S. cities is one of the strongest themes in the stratification literature.

The good news is that racial residential segregation is declining. Based on census data from 1980 to 2000, researchers have found that black-white residential segregation has declined over the last three decades.[1] Furthermore, the presence of other race and ethnic groups in urban cities is important to the level of white-black segregation. For example, some researchers have found that black-white segregation is lower in cities where the proportion of other groups is higher (Frey and Farley 1996; Iceland 2004), suggesting that other groups may reduce the antagonism between blacks and whites, as well as serve as a "buffer" to black-white interactions (Frey and Farley 1996). Other scholars have suggested that other ethnic groups shift the dominant thinking away from a black-white dichotomy (Iceland 2004), thus improving relations between groups. Despite declines, however, black-white segregation remains at overall high levels (Charles 2003; Iceland, Weinberg, and Steinmetz 2002; White, Fong, and Cai 2003). Further, blacks remain the highest segregated group in many major U.S. cities like Detroit (Farley, Danziger, and Holzer 2000), Atlanta (Thompson 2000), New York (Alba et al. 1995), and other cities considered to be immigration gateways (Clark and Blue 2004).

Racial Threat and the Composition of Cities

Just as black residential segregation from whites tends to increase with the size of the black population, Blalock's (1967) theory of group threat also posits that the majority group will perceive a growing threat to their positions and will take steps to reduce the competition with the growing presence of minority groups. According to Blalock, the motivation of the majority group to discriminate assumes two forms—threats over economic resources and power threats. In terms of economic threats, Blalock hypothesized that as blacks compete for jobs, positions, and economic resources, they increasingly become a threat to the economic well-being of whites. Indeed, Taylor (1998) found that the relative size of the black population significantly affects whites' levels of anti-black prejudice and perceived economic threat from blacks. The political threat hypothesis, on the other hand, postulates that as the relative size of the black population increases, the dominant group will increasingly perceive blacks as a threat to their political power and will thus intensify social control to maintain their dominant position (Brown and Warner, 1992; Jacobs and Carmichael 2002; Myers, 1990).

The threat associated with racial competition (whether real or imaginary) inherently leads to conflict between racial groups (Blumer, 1958; Blalock, 1967; Blauner, 1972; Lieberson, 1980). Lieberson and other theorists argue that racial inequality is a product of economic competition, in that whites will attempt to exclude blacks from the better-paying and higher-status occupations (Blalock 1967; Lieberson 1980). In an examination of the labor market outcomes, Tienda and Lii (1987) identified the negative effects of racial competition on earnings for African Americans, Asians, and Hispanics. These minorities faced systematic exclusion from desirable jobs, allowing income disparities between racial groups to widen, even though the proportion of minorities in labor markets increased (Tienda and Lii 1987). Furthermore, the racial composition of areas tends to affect both the degree of competition and race and ethnic discrimination, leaving these groups vulnerable to social dislocation, particularly when there is a shift in the spatial distribution of opportunities and during times of economic downturn or lack of growth (Tienda 1989).

Other researches have linked racial competition to high levels of unemployment among black males in the new economy. According to Moss and Tilly (1996, 1), competitive pressures pushed employers to seek workers with "soft skills," that is, "skills, abilities, and traits that correspond to personality, attitude, and behavior rather than to formal or technical knowledge," particularly in service-based industries where jobs require interactions with customers. These authors claimed that the greater demand of service jobs and workers with "soft skills" may disadvantage black workers, since skills are based on white cultural perceptions rather than objective criteria like education or training (see also

Kirschenman and Neckerman 1991). Furthermore, black males may be at a greater disadvantage than women, since women are considered more adept at interpersonal relations than men (Acker 1990; Steinberg 1997) and the trend toward a growing service sector provides women more opportunities for work (Blum and Smith 1988). Overall, coupling racial competition with industrial shifts in the urban context, the dwindling supply of jobs only increasing the competition between racial groups, further diminishes the chances for minorities to advance economically in a changing local economy. Studies suggest that blacks have significantly higher rates of unemployment than whites and that the racial differences in rates of unemployment became more pronounced during the 1970s as jobs left urban areas, particularly in the Northeast and Midwest (Kasarda 1983; Jaynes and Williams 1989).

What Does It All Mean?

Racial residential segregation, racial competition, and the characteristics of labor markets converge in U.S. cities to affect the opportunities of different groups, thus limiting the pace of racial integration in homes and workplaces as pursuant of the Civil Rights Act. As a result, distinct groups continue to face different social and economic realities (see, e.g., Farley and Allen 1989; Sampson and Wilson 1995; Wilson 1987). Theories of stratification propose that discrimination and competition in opportunity structures are core issues that stratify race- and gender-specific groups in the urban context. To be precise, an underlining tenet in the stratification literature is that structural forms of racial discrimination, such as residential isolation, poverty concentration, and segregated labor markets not only stratify groups spatially but can serve as a source of conflict between them. Thus it is essential to this literature that stratification is examined as a local, as opposed to, societal process. In this way, the literature advances the study of race, urban inequality, and violence by highlighting core conditions present at lower levels of aggregation, such as neighborhoods and cities.

Second, theories of stratification offer avenues to incorporate current race relations in the United States and, by doing so, allow scholars to acknowledge the persistent disadvantaged position of African Americans as a structural feature of urban areas. For example, Massey, Gross, and Eggers (1991) provide evidence of whites' exclusion of black participation in the local labor market and whites' resistance to blacks residing in integrated communities (see also Farley et al. 1978). Stratification theories also reveal the inequalities across race and ethnic groups as these groups compete in the labor force and face differential treatment because of economic restructuring. A striking feature of the United States today is that black employment remains lower than white employment despite the recent narrowing of educational and occupational inequalities. Another important finding is that blacks face greater barriers to residential mobility than other racial and ethnic groups (Massey and Eggers 1990). According to Massey and Denton (1993), blacks remain spatially isolated and residentially segregated from whites at all levels of economic status, whereas Hispanics and Asians have experienced clear improvements as their economic status increases. Similarly Wilson (1987) has argued that blacks reside in areas of extreme poverty concentration, a reality not known to poor whites. The concentration of poverty is largely the result of shifts in the local urban economy, as well as black segregation from whites that results from housing discrimination. Thus, equally important is the emphasis placed on transitions, such as the *changes* in labor market structures and the *shifts* in the racial and ethnic composition of urban areas. In the end, change takes center stage.

Finally, like race and ethnicity, gender bias is built into the opportunity structures within the political economy of urban areas. Whereas criminological theories tend to incorporate gender mainly in family constructs, stratification literature suggests that gender is pivotal to understanding the nature of work, as well as the degree of disadvantage and inequality faced in the urban environment. In fact, as suggested in chapter 2, the lack of concern for gender is a critical issue according to some feminist criminologists (Belknap 2007; Chesney-Lind 1989; Daly and Chesney-Lind 1988; Steffensmeier and Haynie 2000), even though women account for a growing percentage of offenders (Greenfeld and Snell 1999) and also of those incarcerated (Beck 2000). Too often, researchers examine the gender gap relying heavily on situational or individual-level explanations for female offending (Heimer 2000; Gartner, Baker, and Pampel 1990; Steffensmeier and Haynie 2000), ignoring the larger structural forces and gender inequalities that contribute to crime rates. Such tendencies do a disservice to stratification literature that has long found gender to be central to understanding labor market outcomes in local areas (Bound and Dresser 1999; England, Christopher, and Reid 1999; McCall 2000), particularly when one takes note of the ways that gender and race have been accounted for in labor market structures (Browne 1997, 2000; Kennelly 1999; Tienda, Smith, and Ortiz 1987).

While the above points summarize some of the ways that stratification literature contributes to the study of urban violence, another avenue is to illustrate race and gender stratification in labor market characteristics across American cities. Drawing from the stratification literature, I identify four themes that are core features of this literature and display the degree of inequality in local economies using census data from 1980 to 2000. By reviewing these facets of the U.S. urban economy, the salience of race and gender is made lucid. These same themes are applied in the next chapter to trends in urban violence or, more specifically, to the uneven nature of the crime drop.

Industrial Restructuring

Urban areas have undergone significant restructuring since the 1970s, and though the shift toward a new economy has influenced all residents, specific groups have been affected in distinct ways. Although there is no agreed upon measure of industrial restructuring in the literature, I use a measure that takes into account the broad transformation of urban areas from an economy dominated by manufacturing toward a service-based economy (Holloway and Wheeler 1991; Jaret, Reid, and Adelman 2003; Browne 1997; Weiss and Reid 2005). The ratio of workers in manufacturing to workers in the service sector is a broad measure of economic transformation. Low ratios indicate a larger share of workers in manufacturing, and higher ratios suggest that the service sector dominates the local economy. This indicator is disaggregated by race (Figure 4.1) and then by racial and gender groups (Figures 4.2 and 4.3) to obtain a clearer picture of the differential impact that the shift in the urban economy had on distinct groups.

Figure 4.1 shows the degree of industrial restructuring in U.S. cities over time by racial group. The reference line mirrors an urban economy where an equal distribution of workers in manufacturing and service industries would be found. As the figure makes clear, the 1980s and 1990s reflect a time when urban areas were more highly dominated by manufacturing industries, but by 2000 these areas were largely transformed into a service economy. Although the shift in the urban economy

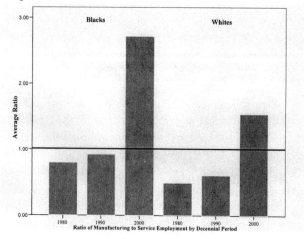

Figure 4.1. Race by Industrial Restructuring, 1980 to 2000

affected both racial groups, the transformation was greater among blacks than whites, as shown in the figure, which is consistent with claims that blacks were more dependent than whites on low-skilled, manufacturing jobs in U.S. cities (Kasarda 1989; Wilson 1987). For example, in 1990 the number of black workers in manufacturing and service occupations was almost equal (ratio of .929). By 2000, however, black workers were 2.5 times more likely to be employed in the service industry than in manufacturing (ratio of 2.66).

Adding gender, Figure 4.2 displays the level of industrial restructuring among black and white males. Clearly black males comprised a larger share of the manufacturing sector compared to white males in the 1980s and 1990s. By 2000, both groups moved into service jobs when the manufacturing sector diminished, but again the shift was greater among black males.

On the other hand, given the high ratio scores across three decades, female workers of both racial groups were consistently found in service occupations as compared to manufacturing over time (see Figure 4.3). The percentage of female workers in service occupations also exceeded the percentage in manufacturing consistently through 1980 into 2000, but the ratio increased with time. For example, black female workers were 2.5 times more likely to be employed in service than in manufacturing industries in 1990, and by 2000 this ratio had jumped to 4.65. The same pattern was found among white female workers: the average ratio for that group was 2.14 in 1990, doubling to 4.04 by 2000. Quite clearly the transformation of urban areas exacerbated the movement of

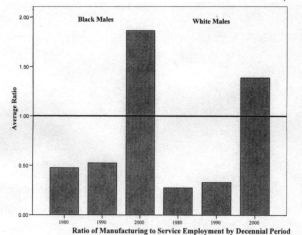

Figure 4.2. Race-Specific Males by Industrial Restructuring, 1980 to 2000

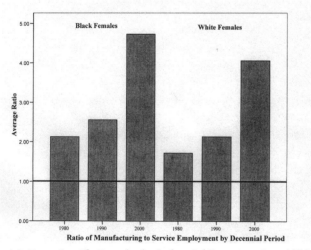

Figure 4.3. Race-Specific Females by Industrial Restructuring, 1980 to 2000

women in the service sector, supporting those studies that suggest that women benefited from industrial restructuring (Blum and Smith 1988). Moreover, the ratios are larger for black females than white females, reflecting the fact that more black females moved from the manufacturing to the service industry than white females (Bound and Dresser 1999; Browne 1997). Overall, industrial restructuring, though indicative of a general transformation in the urban economy from a manufacturing to a service-based sector, occurred at differing degrees among specific racial and gender groups.

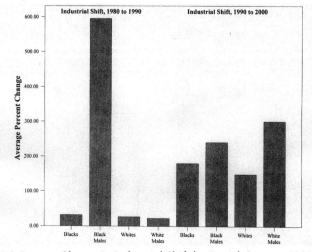

Figure 4.4. Percent Change in Industrial Shift by Racial Groups, 1980 to 2000

To further examine the idea that blacks, especially black males, were greatly affected by the industrial shift, Figure 4.4 shows the percent change in industrial shift ratios for select groups over two periods—from 1980 to 1990 and from 1990 to 2000. From 1980 to 1990 the average percent change in the ratio was 596% among black males compared to 33% change among blacks, 26% change among whites, and 22% among white males during this same period. Without question, the effects of industrial restructuring were most pronounced among black male workers than others, and specifically from 1980 to 1990 than in later decades. The industrial shifts between 1990 and 2000 were significant but more equally balanced across groups. For example, the average change in the industrial shift was 147% among blacks and 181% among whites from 1990 to 2000.

Essentially black male workers experienced the impact of economic restructuring the greatest, and this impact was more heavily concentrated on this group between 1980 and 1990 than in other decades examined here. The economic transformation, then, required black males to shift employment from one industrial sector to another (such as from manu-facturing to service) at a much higher rate than any other group or face dislocation. By the 1990s and 2000s, both whites and blacks were influ-enced by the shift in the industrial mix. In recent decades, it appears that the economic transformation was more equally distributed among racial groups. Overall, these data confirm earlier claims that black male workers were in a greater share of manufacturing than service occupations and, as a result, experienced the greatest levels of employment change during times of restructuring. But moving beyond findings based on 1980 or earlier periods, these data reveal an imbalance in the industrial shift over time. Specifically, black males were largely singled out during the 1980s and 1990s in local economies, where they faced the greatest level of employment instability during this period than other groups. In effect, it appears that the shift in the industrial mix of urban areas—a shift away from manufacturing toward service and information economies—had a larger impact on blacks than whites and on black males compared to any other group. Another issue, then, is how changes in the U.S. economy may alter the degree to which blacks and whites face occupation segregation. An examination of this requires us to look beyond industrial restructuring and focus instead on the specific characteristics of local labor market opportunity structures.

The Nature of Work

While the ratio indicators above provide evidence of industrial restructuring or, more specifically, how the move from manufacturing to service occupations in many urban areas differently influenced distinct groups over time, a separate consideration is the degree to which race- and gender-specific groups are segregated within the local labor market. Though I provide information on the nature of work for race- and gender-specific groups in a large sample of U.S. cities, it must be noted that labor markets tend to serve specific niches geographically and vary considerably by region, as evidenced by references to "high-tech" or "postindustrial" economies. In fact, Kasarda (1992) and others (e.g., Ricketts and Sawhill 1998; Wilson 1987) make clear the regional variation in labor markets. Examining labor markets in such a large sample of American cities, as I do here, can neither account for how some regions are more heavily dominated by manufacturing jobs (Bound and Holzer 1993; Kasarda 1995; Wilson 1987) nor how some multi-ethnic or ethnic gateway areas employ a higher percentage of immigrant labor (Clark and Blue 2004). Nonetheless, it provides an opportunity to look at the distribution of labor in U.S. cities and get a notion of how segregated local urban economies are more broadly.

Table 4.1 displays information on labor market characteristics for a large sample of U.S. cities using census data from 1980 to 2000. From this figure we see that approximately 50% of blacks and somewhat more than half of all whites aged sixteen or older are employed in the civilian labor force. When combining race and gender, male employment has declined over time while female employment increased for both racial groups. For example, black male employment decreased by 6.5% from 1980 to 2000 compared to a decrease by 4.7% among white males. This finding is consistent with other research that reveals a continual decline in black male employment in spite of strong labor markets and economic improvements in the 1990s (Holzer, Offner, and Sorensen 2005). Conversely, women make up half the labor force, and the employment of both black and white females has increased over time. The employment of black women increased by 6.4% from 1980 to 2000, but the largest growth was found among white women, at 10.7%. In line with other studies, the shift in local labor markets actually increased women's employment (Glass, Tienda, and Smith 1988), and white women had the edge over other groups (England, Christopher, and Reid 1999; Kennelly 1999; Sokoloff 1992). Although male employment has decreased over time for both racial groups, white males remain the largest employed group in U.S. cities.

When examining employment trends by occupational types, the decline in manufacturing for all groups and over time becomes widely evident. Again, because of their greater dependency on this sector, male employment decreases the most with the loss of manufacturing employment over time. In the service industry, an industry that has experienced growth since the 1970s, Table 4.1 shows that males (both black and white) were increasingly employed by this sector as they were pushed out of manufacturing jobs. In fact, two notable trends are displayed here. First, males (at least some of them) were apparently absorbed by other expanding sectors (like service and professional/managerial occupations) during times of industrial restructuring. An important point is that although the percentage of males in the service industry increased over time, the increase was not enough to offset unemployment rates for this group. Supporting this claim is that the overall male employment rate decreased over time, even though male employment in specific industrial sectors increased.

Second, although the share of males employed in the service sector increased from 1980 to 2000, white males were the larger beneficiaries of this shift (an increase of 12% for black males compared to 23% for

TABLE 4.1
Race, Gender and Labor Market Conditions, 1980 to 2000

	Blacks			Whites		
	1980	*1990*	*2000*	*1980*	*1990*	*2000*
LABOR MARKET CONDITIONS						
Employment	55.2	56.3	55.2	59.4	61.8	60.7
Males	59.8	58.0	55.9	70.4	69.5	67.1
Females	51.2	53.1	54.5	49.5	54.7	54.8
Manufacturing	32.8	26.2	12.0	26.4	21.5	11.5
Males	49.0	40.3	16.6	38.6	33.2	10.8
Females	16.7	12.1	7.9	11.3	7.9	5.0
Service Industry	22.9	23.3	22.2	11.9	12.1	13.8
Males	17.9	18.8	20.1	9.7	10.0	11.9
Females	27.9	25.3	24.0	15.6	14.4	15.9
Professional/Managerial	16.3	19.1	25.7	26.4	30.7	38.4
Males	14.7	15.7	21.0	27.9	29.7	36.8
Females	17.9	22.7	29.8	25.9	31.9	40.4

Source: U.S. Bureau of Census data, 1980–2000.

white males). This finding supports claims that, even though the demand for service jobs increased, employers seek workers with "soft skills," which disadvantages black workers since skills are based on white cultural perceptions rather than objective criteria (Kirschenman and Neckerman 1991; Moss and Tilly 1996). In fact, this criterion may have lessened the movement of blacks into the service sector over time. It also supports the finding that white males are benefiting from the industrial shift—a shift that marks a move away from manufacturing to administrative and high-skilled information-oriented positions in urban cities (Kasarda 1992).

Conversely, even though growth in the service sector should provide women with more opportunities for work (Blum and Smith 1988), the statistics provided here indicate that black females faced an employment decline in this sector relative to the other groups (an approximately 14% drop in employment from 1980 to 2000). The decline in service jobs among black women may reflect a reduction in the overall availability of low-skilled service and retail occupations as suggested by some researchers (see Goldin 1990; McCall 2000). However, it is difficult to disentangle these trends because only a broad indicator of service occupations is reported here. In other words, this measure does not differentiate retail, low-skilled service jobs from administrative or information-oriented positions. Nor does the measure estimate the extent to which the new jobs created by the growing service sector are actually "bad jobs" (such as burger flipping) compared to positions that require higher skill levels (Holzer 1996).

The occupational sector showing the largest expansion is the professional and managerial positions, although few studies include this category when examining changes in the local economy, focusing solely on industrial restructuring. In Table 4.1 this category includes occupations ranging from top executives and financial managers to legal and educational occupations to health care. While there is clearly a large white-black employment gap in professional and managerial occupations in the percentages displayed here, all groups gained employment because of job expansion associated with the "new economy" over time. For example, the percentage of blacks employed in professional occupations grew from 16.3% in 1980 to 25.7% in 2000 (a 58% increase). By gender, this growth was much larger for black women than men (a 66.5% employment increase for black females versus a 43% increase for black males from 1980 to 2000). A similar pattern is found among whites; that is, whites gained employment in professional jobs by 45.5% from 1980 to 2000, with female workers outpacing males in this occupational category (i.e., an employment increase of 56% among white women versus 32% among white males). Much like the service industry, the expansion in professional and managerial occupations appears to have absorbed workers displaced by other shrinking labor markets, reducing the degree of gender occupational inequality. Although this trend may be the result of employers' efforts to seek "soft skills" or "people skills" in this sector, others caution that the news might not be so good. As Seibert, Fossett, and Baunach (1997) warn, although the distribution of men and women in professional occupations has changed, females are still largely represented in occupations in the health care and educational areas, which are of lower status relative to other occupations included in this category (e.g., doctors, lawyers, engineers, and architects). Tapping the persistence of inequality or disparities between groups is the central focus of the third theme.

Degrees of Separation and Competition

Although too often ignore in the macro-level criminological literature, the existence of discrimination along race and gender lines takes center stage in much of the stratification literature. While efforts have been made to remedy discrimination legally, the empirical evidence suggests that discrimination in housing and labor markets remains a reality among urban residents.

Table 4.2 provides information on the degree of discrimination against, and competition between, groups in large U.S. cities. Using a series of different measures that incorporate characteristics of the housing and labor markets, these data illustrate the degree of, and changes in, inequalities over time. Displayed first is the average level of housing discrimination via racial residential segregation in U.S. cities. Racial discrimination in housing markets creates barriers against improved race relations (Massey 1999) and restricts access to good jobs, public services, educational resources, job networks, and real estate wealth (see Peterson and Krivo 1993). In this figure I find evidence of declining levels of black segregation from whites in U.S. cities. Racial segregation decreased by approximately 26% between 1980 and 1990, and then declined another 7% from 1990 to 2000. This finding mirrors those recently published in a census special report called "Racial and Ethnic Residential Segregation in the United States: 1980-2000."[2] Using all five measures of segregation of blacks from whites, Iceland et al. (2002) found a reduction in segregation from 1980 to 1990 and a further decline from 1990 to 2000. Whereas some segregation indicators suggested that the change was larger from 1980 to 1990 than between 1990 and 2000, as is the case with the index of dissimilarity measure reported in Table 4.2, other indicators of segregation suggest that the opposite may be true. Nonetheless, the general trend is toward a lower level of residential segregation for blacks.

Employment competition between races not only reflects racial discrimination but also taps into the nature of racial antagonisms and the level of racial conflicts in a locality. As suggested by the competition approach, an increase in the relative size of the minority population would contribute to the exclusionary and discriminatory practices toward blacks and attempts to limit blacks' access to higher wages and better occupations (Lieberson 1980). As a result, indicators of racial competition help us to better understanding the degree of racial antagonism in a given area, as well as racial disparities in the local labor market. Based on the indicators of competition offered here, racial competition in employment decreased from 1980 to 1990 but remained steady thereafter, while racial disparities in income levels have grown over time.

Does Racial Inequality Vary across Labor Markets? With evidence of the differential representation of racial groups in occupations presented in Table 4.2, I ask the more interesting question of whether these disparities differ across opportunity structures. Specifically, when is the racial gap the largest in the labor market? It appears that racial differences are greatest in professional and managerial occupations, in that the ratios are much larger than for the other occupational categories. But there is evidence of increasing parity over time, in that the gap has declined from 1980 to 2000 across all occupational categories. Thus, although blacks experienced significant job loss when demand for manufacturing moved out of the urban economy, black workers found employment in expanding sectors in the local economy, decreasing the level of employment disparities between blacks and whites.

Does Gender Inequality Vary across Labor Markets? Asking a similar question concerning gender, the greatest degree of gender segregation is in manufacturing relative to the other occupational types, which makes sense given that males tend to dominate the manufacturing industry. Women tend to have higher employment in service and managerial/professional occupations, as suggested by previous research. Although gender disparities in employment and occupations have declined over time, Jacobsen's (1994) report is a useful reminder of the gendered reality of work. Specifically, Jacobsen finds that at least 51% of women (or men) would have to change occupations to bring gender parity in the distribution of occupations.

Overall, previous research has consistently documented declines in racial and gender segregation in occupations throughout the United States since the 1950s (Baunach 2002; Beller 1984; Carlson 1992; Fossett, Galle, and Burr 1989; King 1992; Tomaskovic-Devey, Mason, and Zingraff 2004), and the good news is that the data presented here suggest that these positive trends continued into the 2000s. Although segregation in housing and labor markets has declined, that there is widespread variation in racial and gender inequality across labor market structures comes as no surprise. This is partly because of the transformation of the urban economy over recent decades, but another likely consideration is the rather dramatic changes in the demographic composition of urban areas. In other words, the location of groups in the local economy is influenced by the composition of urban areas. This link becomes more and more important as the urban landscape

TABLE 4.2
Racial Discrimination and Competition, 1980 to 2000

	1980	1990	2000
DISCRIMINATION & COMPETITION			
Housing Discrimination			
Racial Residential Segregation	72.6	53.7	49.8
Racial Competition			
(Ratio of White to Black)			
Employment	1.17	1.11	1.11
Income	1.59	1.66	1.67
RACIAL DISCRIMINATION IN LABOR MARKET			
(Ratio of White to Black)			
Manufacturing	.871	.851	1.03
Service	.587	.559	.655
Professional/Managerial	1.72	1.68	1.54
GENDER SEGREGATION IN LABOR MARKET			
(Ratio of Male to Female, Intraracial)			
Employment			
Blacks	1.17	1.11	1.03
Whites	1.43	1.28	1.23
Manufacturing			
Blacks	3.38	3.98	2.35
Whites	4.22	4.70	2.35
Service			
Blacks	.693	.812	.863
Whites	.657	.712	.759
Professional/Managerial			
Blacks	.832	.727	.699
Whites	1.08	.922	.897

Source: U.S. Bureau of Census data, 1980–2000.

increases in racial and ethnic diversity. And although researchers have long claimed that the size of the black population shapes the degree of economic threat, influencing the labor market opportunities available to minority groups (Blalock 1967; Tienda and Lii 1987), the presence of other racial and ethnic groups is certainly an important, though neglected, consideration. The final theme that is a core feature of the stratification literature acknowledges the growing diversity in the population composition of U.S. cities.

Population Structures in Transition

The demographic makeup of cities has significant implications for urban institutions, including the urban economy. Quite clearly American cities are among the most racially and ethnicity diverse (Fong and Gulia 1999, 2000). Using census data, evidence of growing diversity within American cities is displayed in Table 4.3. In 1980 the average black population was 18.9% compared to 9% for the Hispanic population. By 2000 the black population had grown to 21.9%, and the Hispanic and Asian populations had nearly doubled (16.9% and 5.2%, respectively). Conversely, the percentage of whites in the urban populace has declined over time, making Farley et al.'s (1978) description of racial shifts in U.S. cities as "chocolate city" and "vanilla suburbs" applicable today.

Mirroring Farley's early work, Massey and Denton (1988) also found that blacks represent a growing proportion of the city population, as whites gradually move to the suburbs. Outside city boundaries, blacks represent only a small proportion of the population. For example, using 1980 census data, Alba and Logan (1993) showed that suburban neighborhoods were nearly 90% white, with blacks comprising the lowest share of suburban neighborhoods. Given segregation in the suburbs and the suburbanization of "good jobs" (Kasarda 1989; Wilson 1996), whites have become the major recipients of better wages, higher earnings, and greater opportunities.

Figure 4.5 summarizes the level of change for specific racial and ethnic groups in urban cities over time. Documented in this figure is the growth in the percent of blacks and Hispanics in cities, as whites have steadily

TABLE 4.3
Change in Racial Composition, 1980 to 2000

	1980	1990	2000	% Change 1980 to 1990	% Change 1990 to 2000
Racial Composition					
Percent Black	18.9	20.9	21.9	25.0	9.6
Percent White	73.9	68.9	60.7	-7.1	-12.8
Percent Hispanic	9.0	11.7	16.9	33.6	84.9
Percent Asian	2.3	4.8	5.2	108.7	8.3
Residential Mobility	40.8	55.7	51.4	36.5	-7.6

Source: U.S. Bureau of Census data, 1980–2000.

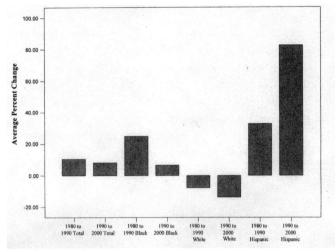

Figure 4.5. Percent Change in Racial and Ethnic Composition, 1980 to 2003

moved out of those areas over time. Although whites in the suburbs benefit from relocating companies (Zax and Kain 1996), urban residents tend to be disadvantaged economically, particularly the black population. Some studies revealed that an increase in the black population was negatively related to blacks' economic outcomes, supporting Blalock's group threat hypothesis offered decades earlier. Researchers argue, in other words, that the declining economic performance of blacks is largely the result of discrimination by whites who feel threatened as the proportion of blacks in the population grows (see McCall 2001; Tomaskovic-Devey and Roscigno 1996). Another explanation proposes that blacks are increasingly placed into low-skilled jobs as the population size increases, subsequently lowering their earnings (Lieberson 1980).

Although the link between labor market outcomes and the size of the group in the population has been well established, we know far less about how black labor market outcomes are impacted by the presence of other ethnic groups. For example, although there is strong evidence of the overrepresentation of minority groups (such as blacks) in industry-specific occupations and low-skilled work (Wilson 1996; Browne 1997; Kasarda 1992), few studies have considered the effect of migration of ethnic groups into cities on black labor market outcomes, particularly in times of restructuring. One exception is the work of Rosenfeld and Tienda (1999), who found that black workers were displaced by other ethnic groups in some occupations but were pushed up in others.[3] Also, often unexamined is the tendency of industries to employ a large share of immigrants in production, influencing the employment prospects of other groups. Accounting for the demand in immigrant labor, particularly given the growth in Latino groups in U.S. cities, is an important consideration. A caution is in order, however. According to Bean, Leach, and Lowell (2004), it would be inappropriate to assume that immigrants are stuck predominantly in low-end jobs. In fact, these researchers found that 26% of adult immigrants had completed a college degree or higher compared to 25% for the native population.

Conclusion

The Civil Rights Act marked a time of great promise in American history. Because of legislative pressures, protections were in place to promote racial parity in voting, housing, and the workplace. And scholars have consistently documented declines in racial and gender segregation in occupations throughout the United States since the 1960s (Baunach 2002; Beller 1984; Carlson 1992; Fossett, Galle, and Burr 1989; King 1992; Tomaskovic-Devey, Mason, and Zingraff 2004). At the same time residential segregation in urban areas has declined considerably since the 1980s, although blacks have remained the highest segregated group in the U.S. Taken together, these trends suggest that race and ethnic groups have made advances both politically and economically since the 1960s. More recently, American cities are growing in diversity as a result of immigration and population shifts. And accompanying these social and demographic changes is the emergence of a "new economy," which some scholars argue is an improved economy, marking the continual growth in information technologies and services.

But what do these changes mean for urban residents? Of particular interest to this book is the link between these important changes and the rates of violence in urban cities. While earlier chapters documented the unevenness in the crime drop and, more specifically, that the rise and decline in homicide rates over time differs considerably for distinct groups, this chapter has illustrated how these different groups are responding to the emerging U.S. economy in terms of access to jobs, sensitivity to restructuring, and the level of occupational inequality that is emerging between groups. The stratification literature has provided evidence of the role that race and gender play in the larger U.S. economy;

thus this literature has provided the foundation for exploring the economic climate in American cities. After reviewing key perspectives, this chapter outlined four themes that identify the ways in which race and gender are embedded in the local economy. These themes document the industrial restructuring of urban areas but also assess the nature of work in these areas, and the disparities that result when labor markets shift over time. The racial and ethnic composition of urban areas was also examined, as the composition of the population has a large impact of the labor market structures found there.

As urban areas undergo changes in the local economy, considerable shifts in employment have ultimate consequences for both whites and blacks. Because whites represented a smaller proportion of those employed in the manufacturing industries, industrial restructuring influenced far fewer whites than blacks in the urban context. In fact, considering both racial and gender characteristics of workers, black males were found to face the highest level of employment instability as labor shifted from the manufacturing sector to the service sector; further, there was considerable imbalance in the impact of industrial restructuring on black males during the 1980s and 1990s relative to other times and other groups. By 2000 this racial imbalance waned even though deindustrialization continued.

A look at the segregated nature of work revealed that male employment decreased over time while women made gains in employment. In fact, even though males moved into the service sector and occupied more managerial and professional jobs, these employment gains were not enough to offset the significant losses they faced in the manufacturing industry. Again, the pattern differed for black and white males, as black males were much more dependent on the manufacturing industry than other groups. To be precise, black male employment declined despite a booming U.S. economy during this time. How might the disparities in the industrial restructuring among black males, specifically the dramatic change in black male employment between 1980 and 1990, correspond to the rise of homicide rates for this group during this period?[4] Recall from chapter 2 that the greatest fluctuation in homicide rates ultimately occurred among black males relative to other groups.

After examining disparities in housing and labor market structures over time, the data presented here indicate that racial and gender inequality has declined in housing and in various U.S. occupations. These conditions provide insights into the nature of race relations in the United States but also inform us of the potential for, and nature of, contact between groups in urban areas. The composition of urban areas has been significantly altered over the last three decades as well.

These themes have largely been unexamined in the criminological literature and have yet to be applied to the crime drop. Although the criminological literature purports that the racial differences can best be understood by exploring the ecological context of urban areas (see Sampson and Wilson 1995; Parker 2004; Wilson 1987, 1996), the commonly used indicators of unemployment and poverty rates are inadequate to capture stratification in labor markets or the segregated nature of the workplace that the Civil Rights Act hoped to dismantle (Nelson and Lorence 1988; Tienda, Smith, and Ortiz 1987). In fact, the short term fluctuations and cyclical nature of unemployment rates make it an unlikely candidate for the more long-term changes in homicide rates over time (see Gould, Weinberg, and Mustard 2002), as illustrated in chapter 2. As we pursue answers to the crime drop, an important starting point, as this chapter suggests, is to examine the changes in the local economy of the cities themselves.

5

Race, Urban Inequality, and the Changing Nature of Violence

An Illustration of Theoretical Integration

Examining the trends in labor market characteristics from 1980 to 2000 found considerable racial and gender differences over time. Chapter 4 established the uneven effect of industrial restructuring on black male workers in the 1980s, whereas economic improvements and a more balanced diffusion of deindustrialization across racial groups signified the 1990s. Although much of the research documents strong regional variations in economic restructuring (Wilson 1987; Kasarda 1992; Ricketts and Sawhill 1988), workplace segregation exists in every region and in all major industrial sectors. In this chapter my attention turns to linking patterns in labor market stratification to urban violence. Essentially I propose ways of relating urban inequality to violence and follow up these ideas with census and crime data for major decennial periods. Some linkages integrate criminological with stratification theories, yet not always. But let us begin by noting a few important points.

First, all connections start with the local labor market characteristics of urban areas. Labor market opportunity structures symbolize the industrial mix in a given area, such as the proportioning of occupations in industrial sectors (e.g., manufacturing, service-oriented, professional, or managerial) within a city, and the shifts in the industrial mix, or economic restructuring. References are made at times to deindustrialization (i.e., the shift from manufacturing to a service-based economy), but attempts are made to expand this discussion by incorporating other changes in labor market structures. A significant point, as demonstrated in chapter 4, is that race and gender inequality is evident in opportunity structures, where workers are often segregated and face dislocation or prosperity as occupational sectors shrink and expand. Thus equally important to detailing segregation in local economies is to document the disparity that exists between groups in the workplace. These facets of the local economy are interrelated, whereby changes in the industrial mix influence the levels of workplace segregation.

Second, I propose to examine labor market characteristics at the city level. Job markets do not fall within neighborhood or community boundaries; rather, city residents are typically exposed to the same labor market dynamics (Bellair, Roscigno, and McNulty 2003; Weiss and Reid 2005; Parker and McCall 1999). In fact, much of the labor market/stratification literature focuses on metropolitan- or city-level dynamics (Adelman, Tsao, and Tolnay 2006; Bean, Leach, and Lowell 2004; Iceland, Weinberg, and Steinmetz 2002; Weiss and Reid 2005). But just because my discussion of labor markets occurs at metro or city levels of aggregation, one should not assume that smaller units (for example, communities, neighborhoods, and street blocks) are not relevant theoretically. On the contrary, I assume that the nature of local economies and the disparities in labor markets experienced by workers are carried with them to their neighborhoods and communities. Neighborhood conditions, that is, are shaped by the larger labor market opportunity structures of an area.

Third, labor market opportunity structures are precursors to other forms of structural disadvantage, such as poverty or unemployment rates, that are commonly linked to violence in the criminological literature (see also Bellair, Roscigno, and McNulty 2003; Crutchfield 1989). In chapter 3 I criticized scholarly efforts to examine the links between economic deprivation (poverty, unemployment, and income inequality) and crime without giving proper theoretical attention to structural forces that contribute to poverty and, more specifically, the vast disparities in poverty levels among distinct groups. The trend toward neglecting theoretical specificity, I believe, is indicative of a larger tendency in the literature to dismiss theoretical clarity when offering macro-level predictors (for examples, see Pratt and Cullen 2005). In an attempt to avoid this theoretical pitfall myself, I propose that local labor market conditions are tied to levels of prosperity or dislocation faced by distinct groups and often contribute directly to poverty and unemployment rates.

Finally, I do not argue that the connections proposed here are the only relationships that link stratification to violence. They serve only as examples of an integrative framework that builds on key stratification themes outlined in chapter 4. Most important, I seek to preserve the structural theme in this book by proposing only ties that integrate macro-level factors. In no way does this exercise at theoretical integration negate the micro-level linkages between employment and crime (Wadsworth 2000), macro-to-micro linkages between labor markets, family, and delinquency (Bellair and Roscigno 2000; Bellair, Roscigno, and McNulty 2003), attempts to decipher the cultural mechanism that connects structural conditions to urban crime (Anderson 1990; Sampson and Wilson 1995; Sampson and Bean 2006), or other attempts at establishing macro-level linkages at the metropolitan (Weiss and Reid 2005) or census-tract levels (Crutchfield 1989; Krivo and Peterson 2004). Rather, these theoretical pursuits at establishing mediating or multilevel processes are important pieces of the stratification-crime puzzle, reflecting the complex nature of the labor markets–urban crime relationship. With these caveats in mind, I offer linkages surrounding the central stratification themes discussed earlier in the book.

Labor Markets, Communities, and Urban Violence

This is not the first time a study proposes to relate labor markets to crime. Shihadeh and Ousey (1998) provide a good example of research connecting industrial restructuring to homicide; Bellair, Roscigno, and McNulty (2003) link labor markets to delinquency in a multilevel analysis; and Crutchfield (1989) offers both micro and macro connections between labor market segmentation and crime. What we learn from all these studies is that work not only helps to structure time (Wilson 1996) but connects people to other social institutions within the community (Crutchfield 1989; Wilson 1987). Work also plays an important role in life course criminology, where scholars propose job quality as a positive transition in one's life, contributing to crime desistance (Laub and Sampson 1993). On the other hand, as argued in chapter 3, few criminological studies allow for the dynamic nature of work, which is central if one is to explain the crime drop. In fact, employment has often been treated as homogeneous and static in much of the criminological literature (e.g., work is good, unemployment is bad). Explicit in the stratification literature is the tendency of labor markets to expand or shrink, altering the economic landscape of urban areas with each transition and impacting communities through the aggregated behavior of residents and the formation of community organizations. By drawing upon the stratification literature and integrating community-based theories of crime, not only are the linkages between labor markets and urban crime made clear, but the ties that bind work to the family and community are made explicit. The three linkages displayed in Figure 5.1 are specifically designed to illustrate this connectivity.

These connections are consistent with the Chicago school tradition and claims made in the social disorganization literature that structural disadvantage can block the development of formal and informal ties that are necessary to promote and maintain social control (Bursik 1988; Sampson and Groves 1989). While researchers have found that structural conditions associated with social disorganization theory (such as family disruption and low economic status) contribute to urban violence (Crutchfield and Pitchford 1997; Krivo and Peterson 1996; Parker and McCall 1997, 1999; Sampson 1987), the linkages proposed here show how labor market characteristics influence the ability of communities to maintain the ties that promote social control, where family plays a crucial role in such a process (Bellair, Roscigno, and McNulty 2003; Crutchfield 1989; Sampson 1987: Shihadeh and Steffensmeier 1994). During times of industrial restructuring, families are less able to maintain networks and participate in community organizations (e.g., sports, volunteer groups, etc.) that promote social control (see Kellam et al. 1982), leading to higher crime. Research on family disruption, for example, has found that divorced parents have less contact with neighbors than mar-

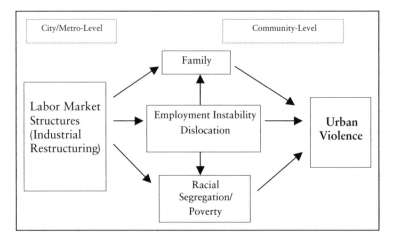

Figure 5.1. Labor Markets, Community Characteristics, and Violence

ried parents (Alwin, Converse, and Martin 1985) and maintain fewer informal networks that assist in supervising youth. The first connection, then, proposes that labor markets work indirectly through the family when influencing urban rates of violence.

Irene Browne's work illustrates the link between labor markets and family, as she has examined the deleterious effect of the economic transformation on minority women (Browne 1997; Browne and Askew 2005). Although deindustrialization increased the number of jobs in female-dominated service occupations (Jones and Rosenfeld 1989), black women lost rather than gained with the expansion of service-based industries (Browne 2000; Kletzer 1991). In fact, as shown in chapter 4, three important economic trends occurred that are relevant to this discussion. First, like black males, black women were more likely to work in the manufacturing sector than white women were (Bound and Dresser 1999: Glass, Tienda and Smith 1988), leading to higher levels of dislocation for this group when compared to others (see examples in Tienda, Smith, and Ortiz 1987). Second, although the economic transformation was undoubtedly characterized by growth in the service industry, much of the growth was in administrative, information-based technologies (see Kasarda 1992), which did little to increase the employment opportunities or advance the economic status of minority women (Browne 1997; Ihlanfeldt and Sjoquist 1989). Third, as noted in the previous chapter, as deindustrialization was in full swing, the disabling of welfare and the elimination of federal welfare entitlements such as AFDC to black women with children who were disproportionately represented (U.S. Department of Commerce 1993) removed any safety net to protect this group from the approaching deprivation.

To illustrate, Table 5.1 documents the shifts in labor market experiences among black women specifically, along with changes in family, using various indicators commonly employed in the criminological literature. Supporting claims made in chapter 4 and previous stratification research, black women were found to be more disadvantaged as a result of restructuring, in that black female workers experienced employment losses in both manufacturing and the service sector over time. Thus, although a growing service sector provided women with more opportunities for work (Blum and Smith 1988), the statistics provided here indicate that black females faced employment decline. This decline in service jobs among black women may have been the result of a reduction in low-skilled service and retail occupations in some urban areas (see Goldin 1990; Hsueh and Tienda 1996;

TABLE 5.1

The Nature of Work: Black Female Labor Force and Family Changes, 1980 to 2000

	1980	1990	2000	% Change 1980– 1990	% Change 1991– 2000
THE NATURE OF WORK					
Joblessness	50.2	52.1	53.5	3.8	2.69
Manufacturing	16.7	12.1	7.9	-27.5	-34.7
Service Industry	27.9	25.3	24.0	-9.3	-5.14
Professional/Managerial	17.9	22.7	29.8	26.8	31.3
FAMILY INDICATORS					
Women & Children on Public Assistance	19.4	16.5	8.9	-14.9	-46.1
Female Headed Households	37.2	42.9	44.5	15.3	3.7
Children Not Living With Both Parents	54.8	65.5	63.1	19.5	-3.67
Divorced Males	8.4	15.6	11.2	85.7	-28.2

Source: U.S. Bureau of Census data, 1980–2000.

McCall 2000). Black women workers have been losing ground in both manufacturing and service-based economies since the 1980s, and joblessness has increased steadily. In fact, even though black women experienced gains in professional and managerial jobs, this growth in employment did not absorb a sufficient number of displaced workers to counteract job dislocation among black females over time.

Browne and Askew (2005) argues that change in federal welfare policy removed the "safety net" for poor women with children, pushing poor women off welfare and leading to rising poverty and unemployment rates (Burtless 1995). Supporting this claim, the data in Table 5.1 reveal an approximate 15% reduction in the percentage of black women and children with public assistance between 1980 and 1990, which drops by 46% between 1990 and 2000 largely because of the dismantling of the AFDC program in 1996 (Grogger 2001; Browne and Askew 2005). This forced many women to enter the labor market, sometimes working below minimum wage (U.S. Department of Labor, Bureau of Labor Statistics 2002) and seeking out low-skilled jobs that were harder to come by as a result of deindustrialization. The adverse effects of labor market trends and the removal of federal aid to families corresponded to the shifts in black female violence between 1980 and 1990, working indirectly through the family. In fact, all family indicators revealed increasing levels of disruption during this time. As shown in Table 5.1, from the 1980s to the 1990s, households headed by black females rose by 15%, the percentage of black children under the age of eighteen not living with two parents rose by 19.5%, and divorce rates increased by 85.7%. On the other hand, family disruption lessened considerably throughout the late 1990s up to 2000, when local economies were rebounding, contributing to lower homicide rates as evidenced in the crime drop (see chapter 2).

Transitions in local labor markets, such as the move away from manufacturing to service-oriented economies in many cities, created a climate of instability for workers as they were forced to seek jobs in other sectors. Times of transition are often characterized by uncertainty, insecurity, and brief periods of dislocation among workers, if not involvement in illegitimate employment (Fagan 1992; Taylor 1999; Uggen and Janikula 1999). Widely evident in the stratification literature is that minority groups face higher levels of employment instability, and the data presented in this chapter adds further support to these claims. To reflect this process, the second linkage in Figure 5.1 shows how high levels of restructuring or shifts in the industrial mix in urban areas influenced violence by means of employment instability or dislocation or both.

Theoretically, this process worked in a couple of ways. First, Wilson (1987) suggested that deindustrialization resulted in joblessness, reducing access to job networks and weakening attachment to the labor force, which increased urban violence. Shihadeh and Ousey (1998) found that industrial restructuring affected white and black homicide rates indirectly through joblessness, supporting Wilson's thesis. Table 5.2 provides data on deindustrialization, labor market conditions, and homicide rates during two key periods—times of rising (1980 to 1990) and falling (1990 to 2000) homicide rates. As shown, the dramatic shift in labor market structures, such as occurred among black males between 1980 and 1990, contributed to rising homicide rates during this period. In fact, as I have argued, black male workers were unique in the degree to which the shift from manufacturing to service-sector occupations created a climate of instability—the percent change in industrial restructuring among black males was 596% compared to 22.3% among white males. As stated, the shifts in labor market characteristics were more in line with the dramatic rise and fall in homicide rates than were other economic indicators, such as poverty and unemployment. Other studies have also noted the dramatic decline in labor force activity among black men during the 1980s and 1990s, suggesting that the employment trends were much worse for black men than for black women (Holzer, Offner, and Sorensen 2005) and for blacks than for to whites (Bound and Holzer 1993; Kletzer 1991).

The work of Crutchfield offers another, albeit related avenue, based on the theory of labor market segmentation first introduced by Doeringer and Piore (1971).[1] Essentially Deoringer and Piore propose that the U.S. economy is separated into two labor markets based on job characteristics—primary and secondary labor markets. Jobs within the primary market are generally good jobs with higher wages, more employment security, better working conditions, and opportunities for advancement through avenues such as on-the-job training. Work in the secondary labor market is often characterized by low wages, low status, and job instability (Doeringer and Piore 1971; Gordon 1972). The duality in the labor market is further complicated by race, where blacks disproportionately work in the secondary labor market-type jobs because of systemic discrimination. Crutchfield suggests that labor market segmentation influences rates of crime where areas with higher levels of secondary labor activity are typically areas with a larger concentration of workers experiencing poor job quality and low pay, leading to collective levels of risky behaviors or higher crime rates (Crutchfield 1989; Crutchfield and Pitchford 1997). The higher dependency of blacks for employment in manufacturing (low skill, low pay) and service-based economies (low status, low employment security) during the 1980s and 1990s, in addition to greater levels of job instability associated with these sectors and risks of dislocation as a result of deindustrialization, led to higher rates of black homicide rates during this time, which supports Crutchfield's (1989) claim that job quality and crime are related at the macro-level.

Just as labor market structures can fuel violence in the urban context, positive transitions in the labor market or improvements in the economy can reduce violence, such as those indicative of the crime drop. Economists have documented economic improvements in the late 1990s (Holzer, Offner, and Sorensen 2005) and criminologists have likened these advancements to the crime drop (Levitt 2004; LaFree 1999; Blumstein and Wallman 2001). Further investigation into the connections between race, the local urban economy, and crime only further supports this linkage. In fact, a consideration of race and gender reveals two important features of the labor market in the 1990s. First, as shown

TABLE 5.2

Percent Change in Labor Markets and Homicide Rates by Race, 1980 to 2000

	Blacks % Change		Whites % Change	
	1980– 1990	*1991– 2000*	*1980– 1990*	*1991– 2000*
INDUSTRIAL RESTRUCTURING				
Totals	32.7	147.2	25.95	180.9
Males	596.1	237.4	22.3	298.1
Females	39.8	80.2	30.7	87.8
THE NATURE OF WORK				
Manufacturing	-14.3	-54.5	-18.3	-46.4
Service Industry	5.9	.14	1.5	14.5
Professional/Managerial	22.3	34.1	16.7	24.6
ECONOMIC INDICATORS				
Joblessness	2.3	-7.41	4.11	-1.81
Poverty	4.94	-9.06	6.53	7.55
Income Inequality	8.8	-2.25	17.9	-4.82
HOMICIDE RATES	11.99	-43.59	-0.63	-17.18
Males	20.7	-39.8	0.09	-26.9
Females	-11.8	-45.4	-16.7	6.7

Source: U.S. Bureau of Census data, 1980–2000; adjusted SHF data.

in Table 5.2, industrial restructuring persisted into 2000, but restructuring was more balanced across racial groups with time. Although deindustrialization was more pronounced among blacks, specifically black males, in the 1980s, the shift in industrial sectors in the 1990s and 2000 equally affected black and white workers. For example, the percent change in black and white employment was, respectively, 147.2% and 180.9% as a result of deindustrialization between 1990 and 2000. This trend persisted across genders, with a greater change among males (237.4% and 298.1% among black and white males, respectively) than females (80.2% and 87.8%, respectively, among black and white females). Second, as the "new economy" grew, employment expansion in other sectors led to employment gains for detached workers, such as the growth in professional and managerial occupations among blacks (34%) and whites (24.6%). This growth reduced the inequality within and between groups. As labor markets were booming in the late 1990s, in other words, the tie between labor market structures in the new economy and urban violence is modified as other sectors absorbed workers, reducing dislocation and the level of labor market discrimination along racial and gender lines.[2] Indeed, the U.S. Bureau of Labor Statistics (2002) reported that unemployment rates among blacks fell to their lowest point on record in the late 1990s. This larger process, inclusive of racial and gender dynamics, aids in our understanding of the crime drop of the 1990s. By incorporating race and gender characteristics into the discussion, distinct racial patterns are revealed that have not been presented previously.

The third linkage in Figure 5.1 acknowledges the role of industrial restructuring in contributing to the spatial isolation of minority groups in the urban environment (Anderson 1990; Massey and Eggers 1990; Massey Gross, and Shibuya 1994; Wilson 1996). Deindustrialization contributed to the social isolation or residential segregation of African Americans in urban cities (see also Kasarda 1989, 1992; Kaufman 1986; Ricketts and Sawhill 1988). Wilson's term "concentration effects" reflected the continued reduction in employment opportunities and job networks among inner-city residents (Wilson 1987, 58), causing the disadvantage accrued by blacks to become increasingly spatially concentrated. Massey and Denton (1993), on the other hand, though agreeing with Wilson's concerns over deindustrialization, shifted the emphasis to the role played by racial residential segregation in the concentration of disadvantage among blacks. Even with notable differences, both perspectives agree that racial discrimination in housing disadvantage black residents, reducing their ability to perform in, and compete for, jobs in the labor force.

The isolation of blacks from whites residentially results in a preponderance of African Americans in specific industrial sectors (Boyd 1998), further segregating labor markets (Ihlanfeldt 1992; Kain 1992). For example, as shown in Table 5.3, the sizable racial gap in employment and labor market opportunities appear in areas with extreme (60% or higher) levels of racial segregation compared to areas where segregation is considerably lower (35% or less). Clearly racial disparities in employment are greater in more segregated areas, and, further, African Americans are more likely to be employed in the manufacturing sector. Deindustrialization is another factor that makes blacks more vulnerable to dislocation and employment instability than whites in highly segregated areas.[3] Moreover, racial disparities in terms of access to professional and

TABLE 5.3
Racial Disparity in Labor Market Opportunities
by Level of Segregated Areas, 1980 to 2000

	1980	1990	2000
RACIAL RESIDENTIAL SEGREGATION OF 60% OR MORE (N=69)			
Disparities in Labor Market Opportunities:			
Ratio of Whites to Blacks			
Employed	1.09	1.15	1.16
Manufacturing	.758	.825	.932
Service Industry	.471	.478	.561
Managerial Professional	1.95	1.89	1.73
RACIAL RESIDENTIAL SEGREGATION OF 35% OR LESS (N=32)			
Disparities in Labor Market Opportunities:			
Ratio of Whites to Blacks			
Employed	1.01	1.03	1.00
Manufacturing	1.24	.935	1.23
Service Industry	.877	.732	.831
Managerial Professional	1.32	1.36	1.22

Source: U.S. Bureau of Census data, 1980–2000.

managerial occupations are quite large in more segregated environments, suggesting that these employment sectors are not available to workers largely because they have moved to the suburbs (Zax and Kain 1996).

This suggests that racially segregated areas are hindered when attracting potential employers, further disadvantaging black workers in the labor market (Bogard et al. 2001) and significantly limiting the types of jobs available. Research has found that areas of concentrated disadvantage tend to have retail establishments that employ fewer workers and offer low pay (Bingham and Zhang 1997). In a study of Chicago neighborhoods, Alwitt and Donley (1997) portrayed poor zip codes with areas that had few large grocery stores, banks, and drug stores, but more liquor stores. Wilson (1996) made a similar observation when noting that the closure of manufacturing plants triggered "the exodus of the smaller stores, the banks and other businesses that relied on the wages paid by the larger employers" (Wilson 1996, 35). The nature and type of businesses found in segregated areas affect the community's level of collective efficacy (Sampson, Raudenbush, and Earls 1997), if not increase levels of public disorder (Greenbaum and Tita 2004; Wilcox, Quisenberry, and Cabrera 2004) because of the abundance of "liquor stores and currency exchanges" (Wil-

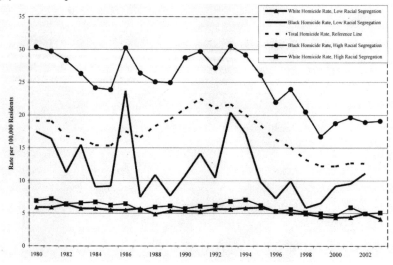

Figure 5.2. Racial Gap in Homicide Rates
by Types of Segregated Areas, 1980 to 2003

son 1996, 5). These conditions increase the attractiveness of illicit drug markets as an alternative source of income (Fagan 1992). And violence associated with illicit drug markets is related to the prevalence of homicide (Blumstein 1995). Evidence has linked illicit drug markets (especially the crack-cocaine epidemic), which peaked in the early 1990s, to homicide trends during this same period (Ousey and Lee 2002). Ford and Beveridge (2004) found that visible drug sales only further diminished the ability of urban areas to attract more desirable businesses.

When labor market opportunities are further constrained by a racial segregated environment, racial disparities in urban violence only follow. Figure 5.2 displays time-series data on race-specific homicide rates for urban areas with extreme and low levels of racial segregation.[4]

As a companion to this figure, summary statistics are provided in Table 5.4. These longitudinal data reveal that the black homicide rate in areas of extreme segregation is generally 2 to 3 times higher than black homicide rates in areas of lower segregation. For example, in 1980 the black homicide rate was 15.3 in areas of low segregation but twice as high in extremely segregated areas (rate of 30.4 per 100,000 black persons). By 1991 the rate disparities in the two area types had increased (rates of 10.8 versus 29.7 per 100,000 black persons). At the lowest point of the crime drop (2000), the black homicide rates in extremely segregated areas was still 3 times higher than those found in areas of low segregation (6.5 versus 18.7 rate per 100,000 black persons). As shown in both Figure 5.2 and Table 5.4, white homicide rates followed a similar pattern. For example, white homicide rates tended to be 1.5 to 2 times higher in extremely segregated areas compared to their rates in areas with low levels of segregation. Further, these differences persisted over time. The findings presented here support the claims made by Krivo and Peterson (2000) using cross-sectional crime and census data that, regardless of race, violence is high in areas of extreme disadvantage. But the data further reveal that the white-black gap in homicide rates was much higher in areas of extreme racial segregation. Specifically, black homicide rates tended to be 2 to 4 times higher than white homicide rates in less segregated areas, but the disparities increased (to a range of 4 to 5 times) in areas of extreme segregation.

Because racial subordination only increased with racial isolation (Massey and Denton 1993), urban violence was also elevated and the racial disparities between groups grew. When exploring the connection between racial segregation and rates of black violence, Shihadeh and Flynn (1996) suggested that the segregation of urban blacks in communities with few labor market opportunities weakens attachments to legitimate labor markets and investments in conventional society while increasing exposure to illegal activities (see also Wilson 1996; Anderson 1999). Crutchfield, Glusker, and Bridges (1999) also found that the impact of job quality on crime is highest in areas of disadvantage. Finally, Peterson and Krivo (1993) argued that racial discrimination in housing restricts access to good jobs, education, and real estate wealth, contributing to higher rates of violence. Thus, although the linkage between racial segregation and urban violence is one of the more pursued relationships in the criminological literature, few researchers have examined the far

TABLE 5.4

Racial Gap in Homicide Rates by Level of Segregated Areas Over Time

| | Racial Segregation | | | | | |
| | Low | | | Extreme | | |
	1980	1991	2000	1980	1991	2000
Black	15.3	10.8	6.5	30.4	29.7	18.7
White	3.69	3.74	2.86	6.89	6.06	4.67
Black-White Ratio	4.15	2.89	2.27	4.41	4.90	4.00

Source: Adjusted SHF data.

more intricate link between labor market structures, social isolation, and urban violence. Similarly, the racial disparities or gap in violence has only gained attention recently (see LaFree, O'Brien, and Baumer 2006), yet the role of racial segregation as a contributor to the racial gap in violence has not been explored. The findings revealed here suggest that racial residential segregation may play a significant role, directly and indirectly through labor markets, when explaining the narrowing of the racial gap over time.

Investigating these links could draw on Mertonian notions of strain, as Peterson and Krivo (1993) have done, by suggesting that frustration and alienation change with levels of social isolation. Another possible integration between labor market stratification and violence captures the long-held tradition in sociological writings (including Marxist, conflict, and strain theories) concerning the impact of economic deprivation (poverty and income inequality) on crime. These theories rely on the notion that deprivation (in relative or absolute terms) heightens feelings of anger and frustration that result in aggression (e.g., violence). According to Blau and Blau (1982), when an economically polarized environment is coupled with ascribed (racial) forms of inequality, the potential for violence increases. It is easy to see how frustration could be elevated by discrimination in housing markets, particularly in light of the rather blatant attempts at real estate steering documented by Yinger (1995). Conversely, as black-white residential segregation continues to decline (Charles 2003; Iceland, Weinberg, and Steinmetz 2002; Logan, Stults, and Farley 2004) and the economy booms, homicide rates and the offending gap between groups would also fall.

Labor Markets, Social Control, and Urban Violence

The conditions that impede the development of businesses and group relations also influence the ability to maintain effective social control (Bursik and Grasmick 1993), influencing violent crime (Crutchfield 1989). Figure 5.2 delineates the linkages between labor market structures, the ability to develop and maintain community organizations, and violence in urban areas. Few studies have examined how labor demand (in terms of the *number* and *types* of labor) impedes social control. Even in cities where there are opportunities to participate in service- or retailed-oriented jobs, communities can suffer because these

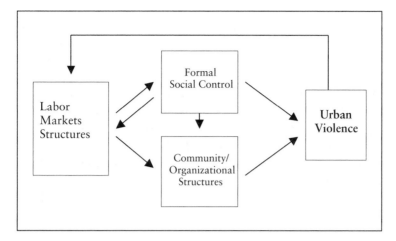

Figure 5.3. Labor Markets, Social Control, and Violence

jobs are offered by smaller employers who lack competitive wages and job security. Wilson (1987) warns that deindustrialization leads to the removal of large employers, which he further links to community structures such as job networks and neighborhood organizations (Wilson 1996). When jobs are absent or undesirable in terms of wages and security, other organizations that bind the community, including schools and churches, also languish. Because important community and organizational structures are tied to labor markets in urban areas, the local urban economy is a critical precursor to violence, as shown in Figure 5.3. Researchers have noted that employers leave areas with high crime rates (Cullen and Levitt 1996). Even low-wage employers in the service industry relocate when faced with increasing crime rates (Weiss and Reid 2005). Thus any linkages between labor market structures and violence must also acknowledge the potential for a reciprocal relationship, as illustrated in the figure.

Another notable feature of urban areas is the greater use and dependency on formal social control. In recent years social disorganization theory has not only identified communities that have higher levels of crime and disorder but have also shown how communities are more dependent on formal social control to maintain order. This is partly because of the breakdown in informal control, leaving communities less able to supervise youth, but also because community members lack the ties to job networks and community organizations that foster social order. In line with Bursik and Grasmick (1993), Rose and Clear (1998) have provided empirical evidence that community dependency on formal mechanisms of social control (via incarceration and police presence) further weakens organizational and family structures, which results in more (rather than less) crime.

Again Merton's work surfaces, because he was one of the first scholars to acknowledge the link between race, opportunity structures, and social control. Merton (1938) asserted that racial discrimination reduces access to legitimate opportunities in the labor market and increases the obstacles that minority groups face; this, in turn, leads to illegitimate behavior, which results in incarceration. The threat thesis offers another connection by postulating that as the relative size of the black population increases the dominant group will increasingly perceive blacks as a threat to their political power and will thus intensify social control to maintain their dominant position (Brown and Warner 1992; Carmichael 2005; Jacobs and Carmichael 2002; Myers 1990). Scholars have demonstrated a concentration of police disproportionately in black urban areas (see Jackson and Carroll 1981; Liska, Lawrence, and Benson 1981) and the rise in incarceration over time (Bureau of Justice Statistics 1996), particularly among black males (Lynch and Sabol 1997). Thus, although the link between race and social control has been well established in the criminological literature (Mauer 1999; Sampson and Lauritsen 1997; Tonry 1995; Walker, Spohn, and Delone 2003), the larger connection between racial stratification and rates of incarceration is another important consideration.

Figure 5.4 displays time-series data on the rates of incarceration per 100,000 population for specific groups from 1980 to 2003. The trend in the total incarceration rate is added as a reference point. Again, an examination of the rise in incarceration for the total population does disservice to the racially disparate nature of federal- and state-level incarceration trends over time. Though rates have increased for all groups, the dramatic rise in the black male incarceration rate is the most notable trend in this figure. In fact, the application of formal social control toward black males, relative to other groups, is quite remarkable. A U.S. Department of Justice (2003) report reveals that the black male incarceration rate is more than seven times the rate of white men.

While incarceration rates were booming, industrial restructuring was also expanding, resulting in a discernable influence on black males relative to other groups. Deserving serious consideration, then, is the link between labor markets, the use of incarceration, and urban violence. For example, a rise in black male incarceration reduces the pool of potential spouses (Anderson 1999; Wilson 1987, 1996), influencing the community

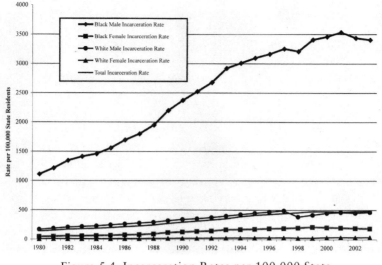

Figure 5.4. Incarceration Rates per 100,000 State
Residents by Racial Groups, 1980 to 2003

level of informal social control. Prior incarceration makes black males more sensitive to labor market conditions, such as poor wages and dislocation (Holzer, Offner, and Sorensen 2005; Western and Pettit 2005). In fact, Holzer and colleagues (2005) contribute incarceration estimates to the downward trend in black male employment rates, as employers tend to avoid black men with criminal records (see also Holzer 1996).[5]

Another consequence is the restrictions on civil rights after a felony conviction, commonly called *collateral consequences* (Wheelock 2005; Uggen and Manza 2002). In addition to losing the right to vote, many states place limitations on other civil rights, including parental rights (where a felony conviction is grounds for divorce), receiving educational scholarships and grants, firearm ownership, a welfare ban, and restrictions on employment and occupations, among others (Buckler and Travis 2003; Burton, Cullen, and Travis 1987; Wheelock 2005). These collateral consequences impede access to labor markets and limit other community activities. For example, based on Bureau of Justice statistics, an estimated 4.7 million people have lost their right to vote as a result of a felony conviction. And, between 1996 and 1999, the welfare ban for felons affected ninety-two thousand women. To incorporate these larger considerations, particularly the consequences of felony conviction and incarceration on parenting, education, and employment, Figure 5.2 denotes the reciprocal relationship (or the cyclical nature of the relationship) between labor market structures and formal social control. And since incarceration is one of the more popular explanations for the crime drop, these larger structural forces and the potential for mediating effects with labor markets are equally in need of attention, particularly in light of the racial gap in incarceration.

Labor Markets and Urban Violence in Multiethnic Places

Finally, I acknowledge that labor market structures can influence the level of urban violence directly. A recent quote from Sampson and Bean (2006) is particularly useful when making this point. They write: "Specifically, neighborhoods where more people have professional or managerial jobs are protective against violence, as are neighborhoods with higher concentrations of immigrants" (8). Not only does this statement signify the direct link between labor markets and urban crime but it acknowledges that the demographic composition of this area shapes this connection.

We are in the midst of a great wave of immigration. And clearly American cities are among the most racially and ethnically diverse in the world. As of 2005, 12.4 percent or approximately 35.6 million persons in the nation's population were foreign-born (U.S. Census Bureau 2005). Large concentrations of immigrants are found in certain states, for example, California, Florida, New York, and Texas, and also in gateway cities such as New York, Chicago, Miami, and Los Angeles, as, in 2005, the percentage of persons with Hispanic or Latino origins reached 14.5 percent nationally. This reflects a growth of 16% since the 2000 Census only five years earlier, surpassing the size of the African American population, which was 12.1% in 2005. How are immigrants finding work in these declining cities of deindustrialization?

According to Waldinger (1996), ethnic groups have been able to establish small business niches in the labor market where African Americans have not. For example, immigrants can provide goods manufactured outside the United States. As Waldinger points out, Korean-owned small businesses in New York city sell wigs supplied by Korean wholesalers or run grocery stores where not much capital is required and yet turnover is good. Another advantage immigrants have in creating small businesses is that they tend to be highly integrated in community networks such as churches and immigrant organizations within their neighborhoods, which facilitate access to information, capital, and workers. Clearly the racial and ethnic composition of urban areas shape the structure of the

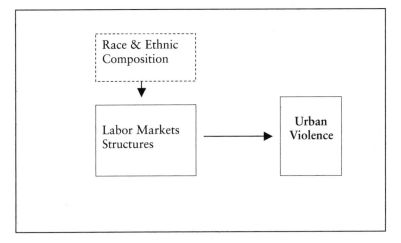

Figure 5.5. Population Characteristics, Labor Markets, and Violence

labor market. Furthermore, these groups face less discrimination than blacks as evidenced in housing patterns and segregation studies (Alba and Logan 1991; Clark and Blue 2004).

Some research suggests that an increase in ethnic-owned businesses boosts the employment opportunities for city residents when white employers move to the suburbs (Zax and Kain 1996). Immigration into the city leads to business growth, such as the concentration of Korean Americans in small businesses (Park 1997). In 1990 Korean Americans had the highest level of self-employment of any ancestry group in the U.S. According to the 1990 U.S. Census, 24.3% of the Korean workforce was self-employed, which is more than twice the national average (Yoon 1997). Korean immigrants are also well-educated relative to other ethnic groups; indeed, 34% of foreign-born Koreans over the age of twenty-five have a college degree, whereas only 20% of all Americans have earned a degree at college.

As cities have become more racially and ethnically diverse, the distribution of groups within labor market structures has also shifted. Moreover, the growing diversity of labor markets may have tempered race relations, lessening the occurrence of violence. There are two ways to consider this connection. First, following the work of Martinez (2002), the concentration of Latinos is relevant to violence, in some ways more so than the concentration of African Americans. Martinez has challenged claims that Latinos are linked to increasing crime rates, a myth that others have also dispelled (Hagan and Palloni 1999). In fact, evidence suggests that recent immigrants and Latinos (in recent decades most immigrants are from Spanish-speaking countries) are less likely to engage in violence, even though they reside in areas of concentrated disadvantage (Martinez 2002). Thus, as the size of the Latino population increases, rates of violence decrease. Furthermore, Latinos and other ethnic groups increase the presence of ethnic-owned businesses and the use of immigrants in both skilled and unskilled labor, contributing to the community. Finally, multiethnic cities can be places where racial antagonisms are lessened as race relations move away from white-black dichotomies (Adelman, Tsao, and Tolnay 2006). As noted earlier, Frey and Farley (1996) have suggested that other groups act as a "buffer" to black-white interactions, reducing antagonisms between them and thus moderating violence. Furthermore, cultural diversity of the population, generally, and diversity in labor markets, specifically, can promote economic growth and innovation by diversifying consumer goods, services, and production inputs (Bairoch 1988; Ottaviano and Peri 2005), which serves to cushion urban violence.

Of course, the opposite can also occur. Yoon (1997) and Min (1996) have provided vivid accounts of conflicts between groups, particularly Korean Americans and African Americans. Yoon, for example, wrote that Korean immigrants "discriminate against blacks in hiring practices, experience frequent clashes with them as customers, and exhibit negative stereotypes about them as neighbors" (1997, 225). Waldinger (1996) also described a process by which immigrants gained access to low-skilled jobs in New York City: "Though labor shortages pulled African-Americans into these low-level industries, they ran into competition with white workers. . . . When the window of opportunity finally opened . . . immigrants had entered the queue behind African-Americans" (138-139). In this way the presence of other groups or ethnic ownership of businesses in poor communities could increase racial tensions and conflicts (see Light and Bonacich 1988; Waldinger 1996; Yoon 1997). Furthermore, immigrants tend to own and operate businesses in ethnic enclaves or serve niches that are within secondary labor markets (Portes and Rumbaut 1996). Recall that secondary labor markets tend to be characterized by low wages and little job security (Doeringer and Piore 1971). These employment opportunities, then, are with smaller employers who offer little advancement and low pay to urban residents (Zhou 1992; Reid and Rubin 2003). With these possibilities in mind, the relationship between labor markets and violence clearly alter with the racial and ethnic composition of the area. In sum, race and gender are "at work" in local labor market structures. The composition of the population, particularly regarding diversity, is critical to understanding these labor market dynamics, influencing the nature of race relations and the disparities and trends in urban violence. As the above linkages and figures suggest, this relationship is full of complexity.

The Crime Drop: A Tale of Two Cities

The complex relationship between race, labor markets, and crime is evident in two American cities: Detroit, Michigan, an "old" industrial city of the North still dominated by a manufacturing economy, and Dallas, Texas, a city representing the "new economy" of the South. An exploration into the local economy of these two cities reveals considerable differences, even though both cities saw a decrease in crime during the 1990s. Let us begin with a brief history.

An Economic History and Background

The automotive industry brought thousands of immigrants into Detroit during the 1920s, but the 1960s witnessed a decline in the manufacturing industry, when more than half the jobs lost were in manufacturing. In an effort to recover, a group of business leaders formed Detroit Renaissance to address the city's future. In the early 1970s, the group, now under the leadership of its chairman, Henry Ford II, announced plans to construct the world's largest privately financed project, the Renaissance Center, as a symbol of the new Detroit. This center, in 1996, was purchased by General Motors Corporation for its new global headquarters.

Despite losses in manufacturing, Detroit remains a leader in the automotive industry. Indeed, it is the world headquarters not only for General Motors Corporation but also for the Ford Motor Corporation, the DaimlerChrysler Corporation, and Volkswagen of America. Other corporations, both national and international, have headquartered there as well, including Kmart, Compuware, American National Resources, and Federal Mogul. Just north of the city is the Auburn Hills area, which is called "Automation Alley" because of the large number of robotics firms that have located there in recent years. Other budding industries include firms that research hydrogen fuel cells and non-petroleum power-generating technologies that may drive the automobiles of the future. Thus the automotive industry that provided work for many immigrants at the beginning of the twentieth century is still central to the city's economic base today. Detroit is the "Motor City."

Dallas, on the other hand, is a "new" postindustrial city that boasts a diverse business climate, with technological industries in the lead. For example, some major industries include defense, financial services, information technology, telecommunications, and processing. According to the Dallas Chamber of Commerce, the Dallas-Fort Worth metro-area holds about 43% of the state's high-tech workers. There are nineteen *Fortune 500* companies headquartered in the area, including Dean Foods, Exxon-Mobil, Kimberly-Clark, Neiman Marcus, Southwest Airlines, and Texas Instruments. Dubbed the "Silicon Prairie," Dallas is among the country's largest employment centers for high technology, and is also known for telecommunications throughout the United States.

Table 5.5 provides evidence of the notable differences in the economic characteristics of these two cities. While Detroit is known for manufacturing and Dallas for its concentration in high-tech industries, Dallas outnumbered Detroit in its manufacturing establishments during the late 1980s. Yet, perhaps more important, an estimated 60% of production workers in Detroit were employed in large manufacturing plants with more than five hundred employees compared to only 25% in Dallas. Unemployment figures reveal the influence of deindustrialization on these two cities, where the unemployment rate is twice as high in Detroit as it is in Dallas (13.1 and 6.9, respectively). In fact, Detroit has one of the highest unemployment rates in the nation. More than 50% of manufacturing jobs were lost in Detroit during the 1970s and 1980s (McCall 2001), and, in the 1980s, Detroit was among the nation's leaders in concentrated poverty and neighborhood distress, faring the worst of all cities examined in Kasarda's 1993 report.

At the same time, Detroit also has a smaller percentage of college-educated individuals than Dallas (9.6% and 27.1%, respectively), and also fewer persons aged twenty-five or older with high school degrees or higher (62.1% and 73.5%, respectively). Researchers have found that areas with a small share of college-educated workers have higher racial and gender inequalities (McCall 2001).

Although few published works provide the history of race relations in Dallas, Detroit is one of the most frequently studied cities in the stratification literature. For example, Farley, Danziger, and Holzer (2000) examined the trends and key turning points in Detroit's race

TABLE 5.5
Economic Characteristics of Detroit and Dallas

	Detroit	Dallas
Number Employed[a]	335,462	511,202
% Manufacturing	20.5	14.1
% Wholesale and Retail Trade	18.5	22.9
% Financial, Real Estate, Insurance	6.2	10.9
% Health Services	11.4	6.8
Unemployment Rate[a]	13.1	6.9
Number Manufacturing Establishments	1255	2105
Share of Production Workers in Large Manufacturing Plants (more than 500 employees, 1987)[b]	60.0	25.0
% High School Degree or Higher[a]	62.1	73.5
% Bachelor Degree or Higher[a]	9.6	27.1

a. U.S. Bureau of Census data.
b. 1987 Economic Census (U.S. Department of Commerce 1994).

relations over three centuries. Racial tension, traceable to a race riot in 1863, labor market characteristics and its sizable manufacturing base, as well as the composition of its population all mark Detroit's past. Facing economic decline, Detroit, like many other larger industrial cities of the North, experienced considerable population loss. Table 5.6 reveals the composition of population in Detroit and Dallas over three decades. As this table shows, Detroit faced a 14.6% drop in population during the 1980s, which was followed by another 7.5% drop between 1990 and 2000. Much of this population decline was the direct result of white flight (e.g., an estimated 42.6% drop in the white population between 1990 and 2000 alone). Although the Latino population grew significantly (an increase of 88.3% between 1990 and 2000), this ethnic category comprises only an estimated 5% of Detroit's population. Further, with blacks comprising 81.4% of the city's population, segregation levels for blacks and whites are high. Based on a special census report on racial and ethnic residential segregation in the U.S. from 1980 to 2000, Detroit's metropolitan area was the most segregated for blacks using the most common indicator of segregation (the index of dissimilarity) and the second most segregated area when all five segregation indicators were considered.[6] Thus, although segregation between blacks and whites has declined in recent decades nation-

TABLE 5.6

Population Composition of Detroit and Dallas Over Three Decades

	1980	1990	2000	% Change 1980 to 1990	% Change 1990 to 2000
DETROIT					
Total	1,203,339	1,027,974	951,270	-14.6	-7.5
White	34.4	21.6	12.4	-37.2	-42.6
Black	63.1	75.7	81.4	19.9	7.53
Hispanic	2.37	2.64	4.97	11.4	88.3
Asian	0.55	0.82	1.0	49.1	21.9
Racial Segregation	73.4	65.9	62.3	-10.2	-5.5
DALLAS					
Total	2,055,000	4,037,282	5,221,801	96.5	29.3
White	61.4	55.3	50.9	-9.9	-7.96
Black	29.4	29.5	25.8	0.34	-12.5
Hispanic	12.2	20.33	35.61	66.6	75.2
Asian	0.85	2.18	2.70	156.5	23.8
Racial Segregation	83.2	65.22	61.89	-21.6	-5.11

Source: U.S. Bureau of Census data.

ally, Detroit remains one of the highest segregated areas in the United
States. But improvements were on the horizon. After many years of
job loss, racial tensions, and headlines using words like "crime" and
"decay" to describe the city, Detroit was deemed the "comeback city"
by the *Chicago Tribune* in 1993.

The overriding association with Dallas, of course, and the one that
lingers in our memory, occurred on November 22, 1963, when President
John F. Kennedy was assassinated in a cavalcade moving through the
Dallas streets. Typically Dallas, though a city of diversity, is not marred
by racial hostility, an uncommon attribute given its southern locale. This
diversity is evident not only in the industries it attracts but also in the
composition of its population. When much of the nation's cities were
facing population loss, Dallas enjoyed unprecedented growth. As shown
in Table 5.6, Dallas's population doubled from 1980 to 1990, only to
increase again by an estimated 29% between 1990 and 2000. Unlike
most cities where white flight was common as the black population rose,

both whites and blacks have moved out of Dallas. From 1990 to 2000, census figures reported a decline of approximately 8% among whites and 12.5% among African Americans. On the other hand, Dallas has experienced a growth in Hispanic and Asian residents over time. Hispanics comprised 20% of the population in 1990, growing to an estimated 35.6% in 2000—a growth of 75% in ten years. Dallas's proximity to Mexico and its international economic climate, home to the fifth busiest airport in the world (Payne and Fitzpatrick 1999), contributes to its population growth and diversity.

The Crime Drop in Detroit and Dallas

Can two cities of such vast economic and demographic differences both experience a drop in violence during the same period, namely, the 1990s? The answer is yes, as shown in Table 5.7. The average homicide rate in Detroit was 59.83 per 100,000 population in 1991, which dropped to 40.72 by 2000, a decrease of approximately 32%. In Dallas, meanwhile, the average homicide rate was 49.66 per 100,000 persons in 1991, dropping to a rate of 20.63 in 2000, an estimated reduction in violence of 58.46%. Thus, although crime did decline in both cities during the 1990s, the drop was considerably larger in Dallas than in Detroit. It is important to note, however, that although homicide rates declined generally in both places, the racial gap in homicide rates diverged considerably in the two cities. In Detroit, the racial gap in homicide offending rates increased by 21.5%, whereas the racial gap narrowed by 36.5% in

TABLE 5.7

Average Homicide Rates per 100,000 Persons in 1991, 2000, and Percent Change

City	Detroit, MI			Dallas, TX		
			% Change 1991–			% Change 1991–
Group	*1991*	*2000*	*2000*	*1991*	*2000*	*2000*
Total[a]	59.83	40.72	-31.94%	49.66	20.63	-58.46%
Racial Gap[b] (Ratio of Black to White)						
	1.21	1.47	21.5%	3.15	2.00	-36.5%

a. Crimes in the United States, UCR Homicide Statistics.
b. Adjusted SHF data.

Dallas. As discussed in this chapter, we can attribute these important differences largely to the labor market characteristics and ethnic composition of these two cities.

Industrial Restructuring and Labor Market Conditions

Table 5.8 displays some of the changes in the industrial base of these two cities, and the racial disparities in labor market sectors. Despite the efforts in Detroit to maintain a strong manufacturing base, industrial restructuring contributed to the rising unemployment rate in this city. Although the level of racial competition in the manufacturing sector decreased over time, racial inequality remains high in both service and professional/managerial occupations in the Detroit area.

On the other hand, Dallas, because of its diversified economy, its high ranking as a site for business conventions, and its status as corporate headquarters for electronics and other high-tech industries, has emerged as an advanced postindustrial city. For example, surrounding Dallas's airport is a large-scale national and international transport system that provides widespread employment and business opportunities. Hispanic entrepreneurs in the Dallas–Forth Worth area have created approximately fifty companies dedicated to moving passengers back and forth between the metropolitan area and Mexico, as well as other states in the U.S. such as California, New York, and Florida. Interstate 35, which runs through downtown Dallas and Fort Worth, is also the major route for transporting goods to and from Mexico, fueling ethnic-owned businesses. Thus Dallas's racial and ethnic composition is an important consideration in understanding the local labor market economy, particularly the city's ability to rebound from the economic recession of previous decades. Given Dallas's high level of educational attainment (e.g., 27.1% of the population aged twenty-five or older has a college degree or higher) and its booming high-tech economy, the racial disparities in professional and managerial occupations decreased considerably from 1990 to 2000. But even though the racial gap has narrowed in some sectors, disparities in employment and access to manufacturing and service occupations has increased over time (see Table 5.8).

Comparing these two cities brings to light some important points. First, no single indicator captures the complexity of racial stratification in labor market structures. Though scholars tend to focus on the most

TABLE 5.8
*Percent Change in Industrial Restructuring and Other Labor Market
Indicators in Detroit and Dallas by Racial Groups*

	Detroit			Dallas		
	1990	2000	% Change	1990	2000	% Change
INDUSTRIAL RESTRUCTURING						
(Service to Manufacturing)						
Blacks	.723	1.18	63.2	.789	2.00	153.5
Whites	.594	1.15	93.6	.627	1.29	105.7
RACIAL COMPETITION						
(White to Black)						
Employment	1.08	.969	-10.3	1.13	1.15	1.8
LABOR MARKET						
(White to Black)						
Manufacturing	1.01	.927	-8.22	.562	1.00	77.9
Service	.829	.906	9.29	.446	.649	45.5
Professional/Managerial	1.20	1.22	1.67	2.37	1.79	-24.5

Source: U.S. Bureau of Census data, 1990–2000.

visible effects of the economy, for example, poverty and unemployment
rates, doing so may lead to a serious misunderstanding with regard to
local economies and the potential relationship between economic conditions and the crime drop. Second, the path inequality takes differs
based on an area's industrial mix and level of ethnic diversity. Each city
is unique in terms of the composition of its population, the structure of
its economy (industrial versus postindustrial), and the degree of the city's
industrial restructuring. All these facets influence the degree of racial
disparities in the labor force and the nature of group relations. Finally,
even though crime decreased in both Detroit and Dallas in the 1990s,
the nature of the crime drop differed in each city, as the above comparison revealed. Thus, as illustrated here, an investigation of the relationship between race, inequality, and urban violence can advance our
understanding of the crime drop. Because race is embedded in the local
economy, a critical consideration in this effort is the racial and ethnic
composition of the area, including the growing immigration and increasing ethnic diversity of American cities.

Conclusion

Drawing on core themes, this chapter illustrates how linking stratification with criminological theories leads to arguments that help address the disparate nature of the crime drop in terms of race and gender. Just as the demographic and economic climate of U.S. cities have changed, making these cities among the most ethnically diverse in the world, how we examine urban violence must also change. One need look no further than the crime drop to illustrate this point. Chapter 2 outlined some of the more popular explanations of the crime drop of the 1990s, only to show that the assumption of universality on which these explanations were based inaccurately reflect the nature of the decline in crime. In fact, white and black homicide trends differed considerably based on the longitudinal data. Examining white homicide rates from 1980 to 2003 revealed a steady, yet modest decline in offending rates over this period. On the other hand, black homicide rates fluctuated greatly during the 1980s, only to decline sharply throughout the 1990s. Thus, although crime rates fell dramatically in the 1990s, marking the lowest rates in American violence for more than thirty-five years, significant variation in homicide trends by race and gender suggests that there is more to know than contemporary explanations have allowed.

By exploring the stratification literature and outlining themes that identified the ways in which race was embedded in local economies, this chapter has attempted to move the discussion of the crime drop toward an integrated, multidisciplinary approach. Doing so required a merger of different literatures, including urban sociology, criminology, economics, and race relations. Drawing from these literatures, important linkages were brought to light between race, stratification, and urban crime. Here I again relied on the contemporary explanations given in chapter 2, but this time they accompanied a larger, integrated framework that accounted for structural characteristics of urban areas. Common to all the connections proposed here was a dynamic approach that allowed for changes in structural characteristics rather than maintaining a static view of urban life. Moreover, because so much of one's life occurs within the boundaries of one's own neighborhood, criminological theories that highlight community dynamics played a central role in the discussion.

6

Conclusion

Much has changed in the urban economy since the 1970s. A look at the American urban poor provides a compelling example. Poverty became more spatially concentrated in U.S. cites, with minority neighborhoods experiencing the most extreme levels. Many urban cities saw good jobs move away, as occurred with big manufacturing employers in cities like Detroit. With the shift from the "old" to the "new economy," the urban landscape has been altered, along with the demographic makeup of cities. We now live in an ethnic and racially diverse nation, such that a discussion of urban areas would be incomplete without an understanding of America's rich multiethnic composition.

The goal of this book was to diversify the discussion of the crime drop to reflect these important facets of American cities. Questioning the so-called universal nature of the crime drop and the current focus on broad explanations, such as the growth of conservative crime-control policies that fuel incarceration rates, I examined local changes in the urban space, such as immigration, labor markets, racial segregation patterns, among others, as contributors to the rise and fall in homicide trends over time. This theoretical pursuit hinged on my ability to illustrate racial and gender disparities in homicide trends during decades associated with dramatic fluctuations; to argue, that is, that the discussion of the crime drop was incomplete without systematically including the requisite racial and gender evidence.

That evidence, the focus of chapter 2, came in the form of longitudinal data involving homicide rates from 1980 to 2003, for distinct ethnic groups and for the total population. Data from supplemental homicide reports were examined for each year over a twenty-four-year span and then adjusted to account for missing data on the race of the offender. Next, annual homicide rates were calculated for the total population, for distinct racial groups, and for racial- and gender-specific groups. To begin, I followed the paths of other scholars and documented total homicide trends over time. The ultimate fluctuations in rates were evident, as was the now well-documented crime drop of the 1990s. In fact, homicide rates declined approximately 46% over a ten-year period, specifically from 1991 to 2000. I then pointed out the trends for the different groups, which turned out to be even more striking. After examining a series of homicide trends for combinations of racial- and gender-specific groups, two important points emerged.

First, homicide trends for distinct groups (blacks, whites, black males, black females, white females, and white males) varied greatly when compared to total homicide rates. The decline in homicide rates involving whites started as early as 1980, whereas the crime drop for homicide rates for the total population began in the early 1990s. In fact, both total and black homicide rates fluctuated greatly during the 1980s, climbing precipitously in the late 1980s before starting to decline in the early 1990s. These significant differences were only detectable by systematically disaggregating the rates along racial and gender lines. Second, the racial disparities or gap in homicide rates has changed considerably over time. When homicide rates were peaking in the 1980s, the racial gap was also widening. Indeed, the 1980s marked a time when black homicide rates averaged from 5.5 to 6 times higher than white homicide rates in many American cities. By 2000, the racial gap had narrowed along with the crime drop, where homicide rates for blacks were approximately 3.5 times higher than those for whites. In fact, the racial gap in homicide rates dropped approximately 38% during the 1990s alone. The narrowing of the racial gap was largely attributed to the sizable drop in black homicide rates, whereby the latter were nearly cut in half, dropping approximately 44% during the 1990s, as opposed to the more modest drop (17%) in white homicide rates during this same period. LaFree, O'Brien, and Baumer (2006) also found evidence of a "convergence" or narrowing gap between white and black arrest rates for multiple offenses over time, aligning these trends with greater racial assimilation. In sum, these figures established the salience of race to the crime drop debate. Although this theme has been advanced by a convergence in the black-white gap over time, a larger question still remains: What factors are driving the changes in white and black homicide trends over time?

As scholars often do, I looked to the criminological literature for guidance when trying to identify the factors driving homicide trends, only to find weaknesses in the ability of criminological theories to account for racial disparities in city-level homicide rates. These weaknesses stemmed partly from a lack of attention scholars have given to modeling change in much of the macro-level research. But there were other reasons, ones that hindered researchers when applying criminological theories to the study of black and white homicide rates. After documenting the inconsistencies in studies of race and urban violence, and outlining some of the reasons for these inconsistencies, I turned my attention to the stratification literature that centered on the nature of race relations in urban areas.

In an effort not to get too deeply embedded in the debate of whether race or class (economics) is the driving force behind the concentration of crime in poor African American communities, I focused on that literature which informed me about the local urban economy. Rich in detail, this material pointed out how race and gender become enmeshed in the structure of social institutions such as the economy, affecting group access to labor market opportunities and patterns in spatial location. This literature revealed rather important and dramatic changes in race relations and the local economy since the 1970s, changes that are critical to understanding the differences in employment and residential patterns for racial groups over time. A detailed examination of these racial trends was the focus of chapter 3.

Specific facets of the urban economy surfaced in my review of this literature, and these were outlined in chapter 4. The discussion centered essentially on two important considerations. First, race relations have improved since the 1980s, as evidenced by reductions in housing discrimination, lessening patterns of racial residential segregation, and a decline in racial disparities in employment. Second, changes in the economic climate or industrial mix of many urban cities had a differential impact on racial groups. Whereas the 1980s was a time of economic decline, when black joblessness was associated with manufacturing jobs leaving the cities, the 1990s reflected employment growth and a shift in labor market opportunities associated with the "new economy." For example, Iceland and Wilkes (2006) reported a general decline in the proportion of blacks and Hispanics in categories of the lowest socioeconomic status (SES) specifically between 1990 and 2000, as well as an increase in the proportion of racial/ethnic groups in managerial, professional, and technical occupations. Iceland and Wilkes further reported that changes in SES affect racial and ethnic residential patterns for blacks, providing support for spatial assimilation (see also Clark and Blue 2004). Evidence of their claims was seen in the data presented here. In sum, characteristics of the urban economy in the 1980s and early 1990s differed considerably from the economy of the

1990s and 2000 with regard to the placement and distribution of racial- and gender-specific groups in labor markets. Evidence of these temporal differences was provided in chapter 4, and four themes were identified as emphasizing important changes both over time and by distinct groups.

This discussion continued into chapter 5, where these themes were linked to the racial- and gender-specific homicide trends over time, as well as to the racial gap in violence. Various connections were proposed to integrate stratification with criminological theories when addressing the crime drop. As changes in the local economy and race relations were correlated with the rise and fall in black and white homicide rates over three decades, some linkages were explained by the rise in incarceration rates and the presence of drug markets, whereas others were related to the theoretical elements of strain and social disorganization. The goal of this chapter was to show the larger exchange between the local economy, contemporary explanations, and criminological theories when considering ways to explore urban violence. Although some would argue that these associations could be made in various ways, simply making the connections was critical.

What follows is a summary of the four aspects of the local urban economy, outlined in chapter 4 and expanded upon in chapter 5, that influenced homicide rates over time and for specific groups.

1. *Industrial Restructuring.* The process of deindustrialization marked a change in the industrial mix of urban areas, that is, the share of jobs shifted in many U.S. cities from manufacturing to administrative, professional, and information services (Kasarda 1995; Wilson 1987). Industrial restructuring, then, signaled a general transformation in the urban economy since the 1970s, which adversely affected many urban residents. In urban economies, where manufacturing was a dominant industry, African Americans faced the harshest blow of this economic shift than other groups. Studies have noted a dramatic decline in labor force activity among black men during the 1980s (Holzer, Offner, and Sorensen 2005) and for blacks compared to whites (Bound and Holzer 1993; Kletzer 1991) during this same period. Building on this literature, I found that black male workers were unique in the degree to which the shift from manufacturing to service-sector occupations created a climate of instability. For example, the percent change in industrial restructuring among black males was 596% compared to 22.3% among white males from 1980 to 1990. As one would expect, rates of urban violence by this group were elevated during this time.

This dramatic shift away from manufacturing in American cities directly influenced black males between 1980 and 1990, contributing to rising homicide rates. White males employed in manufacturing were also impacted but to a far lesser extent because they were not as dependent on this sector of employment. Industrial restructuring forced black workers to transition out of local labor markets, causing instability, as they had to seek jobs in other sectors, or face joblessness, which many workers confronted. Patterns of instability and long-term unemployment associated with few employment opportunities within cities were two consequences of the industrial shift; the weakening attachments to the labor force was another (see Wilson 1987). The results of this shift was apparent throughout American cities, including the rise in urban black violence at this time. Thus, most striking about the industrial restructuring that occurred between 1980 and 1990 was the pronounced imbalance across racial- and gender-specific groups, with African American males most directly affected than any other racial and gender group.

Although industrial restructuring clearly continued into the 1990s from prior decades, two important aspects of deindustrialization during the 1990s and 2000 distinguished it from earlier times. First, the racial imbalance in deindustrialization was rectified; bringing parity in the degree of industrial restructuring was experienced along racial lines throughout the 1990s. Specifically, whites and blacks faced industrial restructuring in similar magnitudes and the economic transformation was more equally distributed across racial groups. Second, as the "new economy" took shape, the expansion in employment in other sectors led to employment gains and job stability, such as the growth in professional and managerial occupations among blacks and whites. This growth reduced joblessness and the level of income inequality within and between groups. More precisely, labor demands associated with the "new economy" reduced urban violence as other occupational sectors absorbed workers, reducing both the level of dislocation and the degree of labor market segmentation along racial and gender lines. In fact, the U.S. Bureau of Labor Statistics (2002) reported that unemployment rates among blacks fell to their lowest point on record in the late 1990s. This larger process of change in labor demand, including deindustrialization but not solely limited to it, helps explain the differential trends in urban violence by groups over time.

2. *The Nature of Work.* Industrial restructuring provides only one facet of the U.S. economy. Another consideration is the degree to which

racial and gender groups are stratified in existing local labor markets. The U.S. is in one of the longest economic recoveries in the last half century, and the late 1990s marked a time of job growth. Equally important, then, is to consider the nature, or type, of this economic growth (e.g., not all jobs are good jobs). Estimates from the Bureau of Labor Statistics reveal that between 1998 and 2006 almost all work (over 95%) created in the U.S. was based solely in the service industries (Hesse-Biber and Carter 2004). Because research has shown that women dominate the service industry in employment levels, any growth in this sector should benefit women disproportionately (Blum and Smith 1988). However, my examination of changes in this service industry indicates that it did not happen.

Though the service sector did experience employment growth in general, that growth apparently was experienced by men more than women. When examining the share of males employed in the service sector from 1980 to 2000, white males were the larger beneficiaries of this shift (i.e., an increase of 23% for white males compared to only 12% for black males). This finding reflects what others have claimed about the growth in the service industry largely involving expansion in administrative and high-skilled, information-oriented positions (Kasarda 1992). Even though the percentage of black males in the service industry grew over time, the increase was not enough to offset overall rising joblessness, largely associated with the removal of manufacturing jobs during this time. Among women, statistics show an employment decline among black females in this industry relative to the other groups (an approximately 14% drop in service employment from 1980 to 2000), even though one would expect that expansions in the service sector would provide women with more opportunities for work. The decline in service jobs among black women may reflect a reduction in the overall availability of low-skilled service and retail occupations, as suggested by some researchers (see Goldin 1990; McCall 2000). When coupled with changes in the federal welfare policy that pushed poor women off welfare (Browne and Askew 2005; Burtless 1995), these structural conditions become an important consideration regarding the nature of the change in black female homicide rates over time.

Along with the service industry, professional and managerial positions also expanded. Although the racial gap in professional and managerial employment remains high, all groups ultimately gained because of the job expansion associated with the "new economy." For example, black employment in professional occupations grew by 58% from 1980 to 2000, yet this growth was larger among black women than men (66.5%

versus 43% employment increase for black females and males, respectively). Similar pattern are found among whites, whereby whites gained employment in professional jobs by 45.5% from 1980 to 2000. Advances in professional and managerial occupations, more so than changes in the service industry, aided black workers, buttressing the negative influences of restructuring in American cities that would lead to higher offending rates among this group. In fact, much of the differences in black male and black female homicide trends may be attributed to these differences in labor market opportunity structures.

A look at the racial and gender characteristics of the urban economy clarifies the duality in the labor market. Although labor markets are clearly segregated along racial and gender lines, shifts in the local economy associated with industrial restructuring and expansions in the "new economy" of the 1990s contribute to our knowledge of the segregated nature of work. Together these two economic developments help us understand the rise and fall in homicide trends over the last few decades. During the 1980s, the higher dependency of blacks for employment in manufacturing (low-skill, low-paying jobs) and service-based economies (jobs with low status and low employment security) caused great job instability, which increased the risk of dislocation and also led to higher rates of black male homicide rates during this period (see Crutchfield and Pitchford 1997). But positive transitions in the labor market and improvements in the economy during the 1990s reduced violence, which was reflected in the crime drop. As the "new economy" grew, the racial gap in violence subsided. Indicative of this trend was the employment expansions in other sectors that led to gains for detached workers, such as the growth in professional and managerial occupations among blacks and whites. This growth reduced the level of inequality within and between groups during the 1990s specifically. By linking labor market structures and urban violence, the connection between these larger changes in the political economy and the crime drop becomes apparent.

3. *Degrees of Separation and Competition.* Racial and ethnic segregation is a prominent feature of the urban landscape (Iceland, Weinberg, and Steinmetz 2002; Massey and Denton 1993) and, as Iceland and Wilkes (2006) state, it "speaks to the nature and quality of intergroup relations in U.S. society, where high levels of segregation are often indicative of the considerable social (if not economic and political) distance between groups" (248). Scholars have proposed that black residential segregation from whites reflects discrimination patterns in housing and

exemplifies the role race plays in society (Bobo, Kluegel, and Smith 1997; Bobo and Kluegel 1997; Massey and Denton 1993). The effect of such residential segregation on race relations is clearly illustrated when examining how segregation affects homicide trends.

It becomes apparent, using the index of dissimilarity, that in areas where black residential separation from whites is extreme (scores of 60% or more), the homicide trends involving all groups are higher, disparities far greater, and the crime drop less pronounced. Less racially segregated areas, on the other hand, have lower white and black homicide rates in general, and the racial gap has also narrowed considerably over time. Thus the decline in racial residential segregation in recent years clearly reflects the changing levels of discrimination in housing markets in the 1990s (Ross and Turner 2005), lessening the disparities between groups.

Racial segregation not only affects white-black disparities in crime trends, but it plays an equally important role in producing racial disparities in other structural conditions, which in turn results in intense deprivation in black communities. When segregation levels are high, racial discrimination in labor markets also rise, and this contributed to the differential trends in homicide rates throughout much of the 1980s. These detrimental effects are less pronounced in areas where black segregation from whites is low. Clearly the nature of race relations, as indicated by the level of racial segregation, accounts for much of the racial gap in homicide trends. Simply put, segregation undermines the economic and social fabric of the area, leaving groups vulnerable to shifts in economic demand (see Massey 1990). Researchers have attempted to show how segregation in urban areas negatively impacts all groups by limiting the ability of urban neighborhoods to attract employers and integrate neighborhoods. Improving race relations, then, is key to reducing urban violence generally, and the racial gap in offending specifically. Racial and ethnic diversity is critical to the process of racial integration. Using 1990 census data, scholars have found that levels of racial segregation are lower in multiethnic areas (Clark and Ware 1997), where the flow of immigrants or foreign-born individuals into gateway cities reduces not only the degree of racial separation but the racial tensions between groups (Krivo and Kaufman 1999; Rosenbaum and Friedman 2001; Alba, Logan, and Stults 2000; Alba et al. 1995).

4. *Multiethnic Context of American Cities.* We know that U.S. cities are among the most racially and ethnically diverse in the world, but

is the rise in immigration and the diversity that it brings good or bad? Since the Immigration and Nationality Act of 1965 was amended, U.S. immigration has surged. Much of the growth in immigrant populations has occurred since the 1980s (Ottaviano and Peri 2005), where the percentage of foreign-born residents has increased substantially in both the total population and the labor force. For example, only 4.8% of U.S. residents were foreign born in 1970, but that percentage tripled to 12.5% by 2000. Rising immigration levels is often at the forefront of political and public debate, causing many people to equate immigration and diversity with fragmentation. The idea here is that immigration brings fragmentation, that areas with an increasing presence of racial and ethnic groups are plagued by poor race relations, economic adversity, ineffective policies, even unrest. This claim has recently been taken up by scholars who assess whether immigration negatively affects the U.S. economy by reducing the wages of native-born U.S. workers (Borjas 1999; Borjas, Freeman, and Katz 1997; Card 2005). Within the criminology literature specifically, researchers have also addressed the association between immigration and crime (Hagan and Palloni 1999; Martinez 2002), exploring whether immigration contributes to an increase in crime. The cumulative result of this research is that the concerns over immigration are largely incorrect. In fact, Hagan and Palloni (1999) have suggested that although immigration has figured prominently in explanations of crime rates, it is largely a myth.

Can ethnic diversity, particularly at high levels, then, be beneficial to urban communities? Many economists have long considered diversity valuable both in terms of consumption and production (Quigley 1998; Glaeser and Mare 2001). Cultural diversity such as Chinese markets, Italian restaurants, Korean wigs, Russian ballets, German breweries, Mexican eateries, to name only a few examples, serves the urban economy well by influencing both local production and consumption. In this way, immigration actually contributes to the urban economy, creating jobs in the inner cities and promoting economic growth and product expansion. Still, some people continue to believe that immigrants take jobs away from native-born U.S. residents. There is a growing body of research examining the impact of immigration on the U.S. labor market, particularly native-born workers. David Card's work, most notably, has examined the wages and reactions of native U.S. workers to the presence of new immigrants (Card 2005; Card and DiNardo 2000). Although no consensus has surfaced from this literature, evidence of a "relative effect" has been found; that is, although immigrants may cause wages to decrease in low-skilled jobs, they cause wages to rise in jobs requiring intermediate skills. Moreover, when skill levels of immigrant and native-born workers are similar, with both employed in high-skilled jobs, the impact of immigration on the wages of U.S.-born workers is positive. Ottaviano and Peri (2005) have found that cultural diversity is positively correlated with the average wage received by U.S.-born workers. Scholars have also considered the impact of the size of other ethnic groups on improving patterns of racial residential segregation. Much of this research has shown that the diversity immigration brings to the urban population, and increasingly the suburbs (Logan, Alba, and Zhang 2002; Horton 1995; Marcuse 1997), has had a positive impact on race relations.

These important findings were addressed in chapters 4 and 5 in relation to the crime drop. By examining the rise in Asian and Hispanic populations in many U.S. cities over time, a connection was drawn between increasingly diversified urban populations and the crime drop. These linkages drew on Martinez's (2002) work, among other studies, which found that Latinos are less likely to engage in violence, particularly recent immigrants. An examination of the stratification literature revealed that multiethnic cities have fewer racial antagonisms (Adelman, Tsao, and Tolnay 2006; Frey and Farley 1996) and diversified labor market structures (Bairoch 1988; Ottaviano and Peri 2005), which translate into less urban violence. Overall, immigration diversifies American cities, improving racial and ethnic relations, and also promotes ethnic-owned businesses that serve to reduce violence by creating jobs and contributing to community organizations. These four critical facets of American cities that have existed since the 1970s help us better understand the uneven nature of the crime drop and the dynamic process by which disaggregated homicide rates rise and fall over time.

Public Policy

A discussion of the role that race and the urban economy plays in the crime drop debate is not complete without some understanding of the public policies that affect race relations and economic production. In 1942 only 42% of whites supported school desegregation, but by 1993 this figure had increased to 95% (Bobo and Smith 1994). Although the ways to categorize racial groups has expanded over time (Hirschman, Richard, and

Farley 2000; National Research Council 2004), few Americans endorse categorical opinions about racism or the biological inferiority of African Americans (Bobo, Kluegel, and Smith 1997). Even with these important historic advances, there remains a lack of public support for governmental programs that aggressively combat discrimination, such as preventing job discrimination (Bobo and Kluegel 1997; Kluegel 1999). Here a brief look at the racial issues influencing the crime drop is warranted.

Housing Discrimination

Greater enforcement of the Fair Housing Act, initiated in 1969, is needed to reduce housing discrimination and increasingly diversify the U.S. population by promoting the "suburbinization" of various racial and ethnic groups. Fong and Shibuya (2000) have shown that a higher proportion of suburban residents are Asians compared to Hispanics and blacks (Alba et al. 1999). In fact, they estimated that, in 1990, 49% of Asians resided in the suburbs. There is considerable variation in the percentage of Hispanics sharing neighborhoods with whites in the suburbs, where whites have been found to share neighborhoods with Mexicans more often than with Cubans (Alba and Logan 1993). Alba and Logan conclude that some of this variation may result from the residential preference of Cubans to cluster spatially, a finding supported by others (Logan, Alba, and Zhang 2002). For some groups, in other words, "ethnic communities" are desirable neighborhoods, offering a spatial clustering of ethnic groups with higher levels of education, mobility, and economic resources.

In comparison, blacks comprise the lowest proportion of suburban residents (Alba and Logan 1993), and, in both the suburbs and the inner cities, blacks face the greatest racial residential segregation (Iceland 2004; Clark and Blue 2004). Segregation of blacks is associated with the rise in poverty among African Americans, and, as already noted, segregation is linked to black homicide rates and the widening of the racial gap in offending. Segregation also intensifies economic decline, reducing access to professional and managerial occupations and other desirable, secure jobs. African Americans have historically been unable to convert economic gains into residential outcomes, and scholars have consistently documented that housing discrimination against African Americans is much higher than it is for other racial and ethnic groups (Alba and Logan 1991; Massey and Denton 1993).

The Fair Housing Act, though requiring greater enforcement, did accomplish a drop in the formal barriers to integration, essentially declaring it unlawful for the housing market to discriminate on the basis of race, color, religion, or national origin. Amendments to the act in 1988 only strengthened its effect on housing transactions, and this positive result continues over time. In fact, recent research has found that discrimination in rental and owner-occupied housing markets declined substantially in the 1990s (Ross and Turner 2005). Also contributing to this decline in discrimination is the Community Reinvestment Act which helps minorities buy homes in predominantly white neighborhoods (Friedman and Squires 2005). Thus, with both continued and additional enforcement of fair housing laws and other initiatives, racial and ethnic integration in urban areas may indeed become a reality.

Immigration

The civil rights movement, in striking down racist provisions that allowed immigration to the U.S. from Western Europe while keeping out Asians and Eastern Europeans, led to great change in immigration laws. The 1970s marked a time when immigrants from Asia and Latin America were welcomed into the U.S. And though a century ago most immigrants lacked financial resources, today immigrants are more diverse, typically enjoying higher educational levels, human capital, and ethnic commodities that have given them a niche in the labor market (Logan, Alba, and Zhang 2002: Nee and Sanders 2001). Examples include Chinese developers in Los Angeles (Horton 1995), immigrants and investors from Taiwan and Hong Kong, and Korean-owned businesses in New York (Waldinger 1996). Scholars have related the diversity of the urban population to economic success in many major cities. Sassen (1994) has correlated cultural diversity with economic innovation and growth in cities like London, Paris, New York, and Tokyo. Bob Johnstone (1999) has found that diverse cities tend to be populated by creative people who attract high-tech and research-oriented industries. Although traditional wisdom would have us believe that areas with diverse populations are more fragmented, which stiffens economic growth and the area's ability to invest in local institutions, research does not fully support this logic. Recent studies have shown that cultural diversity and ethnic pluralism is not harmful to economic growth (see Lian and Oneal 1997) and may even promote residential integration. Because the current political climate and immigration policies impede these largely positive and important aspects of immigration, future research must aid our understanding of the role immigration plays in the larger economic and social climate of urban areas. This call for research will require scholars to move beyond the current black-and-white dichotomy that bounds much of the literature. For example, homicide trends of certain racial and ethnic groups could not be included in this book because systematic data on these groups over the three decades examined is nonexistent. Yet, as we face the important challenge of diversifying our research to incorporate a multiethnic approach, we must continue to respond to the long-standing inequality and structural dislocation of marginalized groups in our society, especially African Americans. In the words of Offner and Holzer (2002), let us not forget the fate of the "Forgotten Men."

With racial segregation declining, the urban economy strengthening, and the crime rate notably dropping, black male homicide rates remain higher than other groups. One reason, as discussed in depth in this book, is that black males were hit the hardest by industrial restructuring. As manufacturing jobs moved out of the cities, African Americans comprised a substantially large proportion of the unskilled workers (Wilson 1996; Offner and Holzer 2002). And though there has been a sharp increase in recent years in the percentage of blacks working in skilled jobs (as managers, professionals, and technicians, for example), African Americans continue to comprise a disproportionate percentage of the unskilled labor force relative to other groups (Wilson 1987, 1996). Moreover, the demand for unskilled labor continues to decrease over time (Schwartzman 1997).

Recall that black male employment steadily decreased despite employment gains in the service industry and in professional and managerial occupations, not to mention the economic improvements of the 1990s. These significant trends are related to the rise and fall in urban violence over time. It is important to note, furthermore, that even though crime rates have declined, the rate of incarceration of black males has soared (Wacquant 2000). Along with rising incarceration rates, the role of black men in the urban community has declined. Black men have a 28.5% chance of incarceration at some point in their life (U. S. Department of Justice 2003). And upon their return to the community, they face disenfranchisement (Behrens, Uggen, and Manza 2003; Uggen and Manza 2002). It has been estimated that 38% of those persons banned from voting are black (Uggen and Manza 2002). In some states, typically southern states with a high proportion of black residents, up to 40% of black men may permanently lose their right to vote (Mauer 2003). Incarceration, of course, also limits the employment prospects of many black males (Western and Pettit 2000, 2005), as employers are clearly reluctant to hire men with prison records (Holzer, Offner, and Sorensen 2005; Holzer 1996).

The greatest challenge facing researchers and public policy today may not be the effect of immigration and ethnic diversity on the U.S. population but rather how to address the historic and long-standing inequality that looms large over black males.

Technical Appendix

Computation of Measures

This section highlights some basic computations of the measures offered in the book. Throughout the chapters, an indicator might be based on the total population, a racial-specific group, or a racial- and gender-specific group. Information on the level of disaggregation is given in the specific figures and tables. In all measures, the city is the unit of analysis. The supplemental homicide reports are drawn from data collected by Fox (2005), as published by the Inter-university Consortium for Political and Social Research (ICPSR). Most of the other indicators use data from the U.S. Census Bureau. Some figures present published data from the Bureau of Labor Statistics or the Bureau of Justice, as specified in the figure or table.

Adjustment for Missing Homicide Data

The disaggregated homicide rates have been adjusted for missing data. The importance of adjusting homicide counts for missing data cannot be understated, particularly regarding missing information on race. My previous published works used 1980 and 1990 supplemental homicide data; the adjusted race-specific homicide rates were provided to me by Kirk Williams, who, at the time, was on the faculty of the University of Colorado, Department of Sociology. Kirk, with the help of the University of Colorado's Center for the Study and Prevention of Violence, provided Patricia McCall and me with adjusted counts for multiple years throughout the 1980s and early 1990s. These counts were adjusted based on the procedure outlined in Williams and Flewelling (1987) for adjusting Supplemental Homicide Report (SHR) data to estimate for missing data commonly found in these official statistics.

When it came time to write this book, I needed adjusted homicide counts starting in 1980 and continuing into the 2000s. I turned to my good friend and collaborator, Patty McCall. Patty took the lead, in fact she did all the work, in writing the syntax for the adjustment procedure based on Williams and Flewelling's method. After reviewing previously published work outlining the method (Williams and Flewelling 1987; Flewelling 2004), as well as engaging Flewelling in a few conversations, Patty generated a set of algorithms to impute missing data and estimate race-adjusted homicide counts by considering the distribution of the known characteristics of the homicide cases based on the victim's race, the offender's race, and the circumstances of the homicide. Thus our imputation procedure differed from Williams and Flewelling's original formula, because its adjustment is based on three sources of information. With our procedure, in other words, we can redistribute cases with missing information on the offender or victim or both (whereas previous research only redistributed cases with missing information on the offender). The algorithms were used to calculate race-adjusted homicide data for the twenty-four-year period that is the focus of this book.

The adjustment method uses annual supplemental homicide counts compiled by Fox (2005) and made available from ICPSR; the data from ICPSR are already weighted so that the homicide counts match the Uniform Crime Report estimates for murder and non-negligent manslaughter which correct for underreporting from police agencies. The imputation method is used only on single-offender, single-victim data involving murder and non-negligent manslaughter. All multiple offender/victim incidents were removed. Cases with known information for single-offender homicides found in the Supplemental Homicide Report were used to impute missing data on the race of the victim and the offender for those homicides. Details available regarding the circumstances (or motive) of the homicide were also used to impute the race of the victim and offender. Other details regarding the imputation procedure are available upon request.

Computation of Homicide Rates

Homicide rates are typically calculated by dividing the number of homicide events by the city population and then, for standardization, multiplying this value by 100,000 persons. Because this book required annual disag-

gregated homicide rates, 1998 homicide rates based on decennial population estimates (e.g., 1990 or 2000) would be flawed because the decennial
estimate might not be a good approximation of the intercensal population.
Therefore, the calculation of homicide rates for intercensal years employ
population estimates that are computed based on a linear interpolation of
the enumerated population statistics for decennial years. The population
estimates generated from this interpolation between the decennial census
periods were used to compute each of the intercensal homicide rates. This
procedure made it possible to calculate annual total, racial-, and racial-
and gender-specific homicide rates over a twenty-four-year period.

Change Scores

All change scores are based on the same calculation. The percentage
change is measured as:

((t minus (t-1), divided by (t-1) and multiplied by 100).

Economic Measures. Joblessness takes into account the percentage of the
population not employed and differs from the unemployment rate. Persons are officially classified as "unemployed" if they do not have a job
but have actively looked for work in the prior four weeks and are currently available for work. Joblessness includes individuals in the population not covered by the unemployment rate, in that those persons in the
population not actively seeking work are incorporated into the measure,
which reflects the larger theoretical concerns of Wilson (1987) about the
responses of persons to the removal of employment opportunities in the
urban environment. Joblessness, in other words, is a measure that more
accurately accounts for the percentage of the population out of the labor
force (Wilson 1987). Poverty is the percentage of the population living
below the poverty level. Income inequality is based on the Gini Index
of Income Concentration. In various figures, the unemployment rate
includes the above-defined individuals.

Industrial Restructuring and Labor Market Indicators. Various measures
of labor market and industrial restructuring are included. A measure
called "industrial restructuring" is the ratio of manufacturing to service
employment for specific groups. "Industrial shift" is the percent change
in the industrial restructuring ratio.

LABOR MARKET SECTORS

Data on manufacturing, service, and professional/managerial occupational positions are included in the book. See the U.S. Bureau of Census for detailed information on industrial codes and occupational categories that fall within each of these major sectors. The percent employed is the percentage of persons employed in the civilian labor market out of the total population aged sixteen and older.

RACIAL COMPETITION

Competition is measured through the ratio of white to black in the specified categories, such as employed, median income levels.

RACIAL RESIDENTIAL SEGREGATION

Segregation patterns are based on the index of dissimilarity. This index is a widely used indicator of evenness in the distribution of two racial groups (in this research blacks and whites) across census tracts within a city. This measure is denoted as:

$$D_{bw} = [.5(\Sigma \, (|b_j / B) - (w_j / W)|)] * 100$$

where b_j and w_j are the population totals for blacks and whites, respectively, in a census tract j; and B and W are population totals for blacks and whites in the city.

RACIAL DISCRIMINATION

Ratio indicators of white to black employment in specific labor market sectors, such as manufacturing, the service sector, and professional/managerial occupations.

GENDER SEGREGATION

Gender segregation is the ratio of males to females employed or participating in labor market sectors, including the ratio of males to females in manufacturing, the service sector, and professional/managerial occupations.

RACIAL INEQUALITY

Racial inequality is measured by the ratio of white to black median family income; the ratio of white to black median years of schooling attained by those persons aged twenty-five and older; and the ratio of black unemployment rates to white unemployment rates.

RACIAL COMPOSITION

Percent black: people who classify themselves in the census as black or African American out of the total population

Percent white: people who classify themselves as white or Caucasian in the census out of the total population

Percent Hispanic: people who classify themselves in one of the specific Hispanic or Latino categories listed in the census out of the total population

Percent Asian: those who self-identify as Asian out of the total population

FAMILY INDICATORS

Women and children on public assistance: percentage of race-specific, female-headed households receiving public assistance payments

Female-headed households take into account the number of females maintaining a household with no husband present out of the total number of households.

Percent children aged eighteen and younger not living with both parents is the percentage of children aged eighteen years or younger living in households where neither parent is living out of the total number of children aged eighteen or younger in households.

Divorced males is a race-specific indicator of the number of divorced males out of the total number of race-specific males aged fifteen years or older.

Notes

NOTES TO CHAPTER 1

1. See http: //www.ojp.usdoj.gov/bjs/homicide/homtrnd.htm.

2. The words "Hispanic" or "Latino" are useful examples. When discussing the formation of "ethnic communities" and "immigrant enclaves" in a seminar on race and crime, a Ph.D. student said, "In my home country of Puerto Rico, the word 'Hispanic' would never be used. We're Puerto Ricans, not Hispanics or Latinos. We just don't define ourselves in that way."

NOTES TO CHAPTER 2

1. The Brady Handgun Violence Prevention Act of 1993 instituted strict requirements and background checks before a gun could be purchased.

2. Lott and Mustard (1997) showed that self-protection in the form of carrying concealed weapons and purchasing Lojack (an auto-theft prevention device) lowered crime. This research was supported by Ayres and Levitt (1998).

NOTES TO CHAPTER 3

1. Bursik (1988) and Byrne and Sampson (1986) offer a number of reasons to explain why social disorganization theory was marginalized in criminology during the 1970s.

2. The study of race-specific homicide has grown in popularity, for example, the number of studies has doubled since 1999. Parker, McCall, and Land (1999) reviewed fourteen studies examining race-specific homicide rates and offered a number of methodological reasons for the inconsistencies across studies. The number is well over twenty-eight studies to date.

3. I must acknowledge that a number of factors influence R^2 values, which suggests that any conclusions drawn based on a simply comparison should be

viewed with caution. Furthermore, R² values can have different meanings over estimators, such as the case with Poisson-based modeling procedures.

4. In this table and throughout the book, the computation of the change score measure is the same; that is, the percentage of change in each measure is derived from t minus $(t - 1)$, divided by $(t - 1)$, and multiplied by 100.

5. Fair-housing audits, for example, are another important tool for measuring the incidence of racial discrimination in the housing market, because it allows researchers to define less favorable treatment by real estate agents based solely on the customer's minority status (Ondrich, Ross, and Yinger 2000; Yinger 1995).

6. In fact, LaFree and Drass (1996) indicated that they could not find a single time-series study that included a measure of income inequality (see page 616 of their article), yet unemployment had been used in previous longitudinal studies of crime.

7. Measures of racial inequality continue to be problematic in longitudinal designs. Both LaFree and Drass (1996) and Messner, Raffalovich, and McMillan (2001) report that racial inequality is unrelated to changes in arrest rates for whites and blacks.

NOTES TO CHAPTER 4

1. Some researchers have found that black segregation is decreasing while the levels of segregation have increased for Asians and Hispanics (Charles 2003; Iceland et al. 2002; Logan et al 2004).

2. Available at www.census.gov/hhes/www/housing/resseg/pdftoc.html.

3. My finding of lower levels of racial disparities in various occupational categories over time supports this research (see Table 4.2).

4. Supporting my claim, Wilson (1996) speculated that changes in wages and industrial restructuring could explain the increasing crime rates of the 1980s.

NOTES TO CHAPTER 5

1. My discussion of labor markets reflects different occupational sectors in a city, that is, the level of industrial mix; thus my conception of labor market structures does not depend on these two classifications. This is partly because one type of occupational sector (such as the service sector) can have jobs characterized both as primary (high-tech, administrative) and secondary (retail, burger-flipping). And given my interest in the dynamic nature of labor markets, it is important to examine the changes in specific occupational sectors over time, particularly how these occupations are changing with regard to racial and

gender occupational segregation, which might be masked in a dual labor market scheme. The idea of labor market segmentation, however, is highly relevant to this discussion, particularly the link between job quality and crime.

2. I wish to emphasize that industrial restructuring clearly had a deleterious effect on urban areas, contributing to higher rates of urban violence, particularly among black males, as often claimed in the criminological literature (e.g., Shihadeh and Ousey 1996, 1998; Parker 2004). However, a look at industrial restructuring alone does not provide a full understanding of the connection between racial stratification and urban crime, and nor does an examination of black crime rates without some understanding of the rates and trends of other groups. I contend that industrial restructuring contributed to black (specifically male) homicide rates during the 1980s and 1990s, because this group was largely singled out during the removal of manufacturing and low-skilled occupations during deindustrialization. Black males faced more pronounced levels compared to any other groups during this period. However, during the late 1990s and 2000, the economy improved even though the process of deindustrialization continued in many urban cities. As a result, improvements in the local economy created more employment opportunities for those workers displaced by the move to a postindustrial economy. Furthermore, and importantly, the restructuring of the late 1990s differed from earlier decades in that it was citywide, impacting whites and blacks alike, reducing racial disparities in labor market experiences, and allowing workers to be absorbed into other sectors. This process effectively reduced the levels of urban violence. Thus, beyond deindustrialization is the degree to which shifts in labor markets influence the degree of racial disparities and discrimination in the urban environment. This more comprehensive view of labor market structures is needed in order to fully understand the changing nature of urban violence and the more recent crime drop in U.S. cities.

3. This discussion relates also to "skill mismatch," as discussed in chapter 4.

4. As a reference point, the mean homicide rate for the larger sample of cities was 22.52 in 1991 and 12.18 in 2000. The average percent change from 1991 to 2000 was -45.9%. Specifically, for a large sample of U.S. cities, the mean crime drop was 45.9 percent.

5. Another interesting and important caveat brought to light by Holzer, Offner, and Sorensen (2005) is that incarcerating black males increased employment rates because these men were now eliminated from the pool on which employment rates were based.

6. Available at www.census.gov/hhes/www/housing/resseg/pdftoc.html

References

Acker, Joan. 1990. Hierarchies, Jobs, Bodies: A Theory of Gendered Organizations. *Gender and Society* 4: 139–158.

Acoca, Leslie. 1998. Outside/Inside: The Violation of American Girls at Home, on the Streets, and in the Juvenile Justice System. *Crime and Delinquency* 44: 561–589.

Adelman, Robert M., Hui-shien Tsao, and Stewart E. Tolnay. 2006. Occupational Disparity in a Migrant Metropolis: A Case Study of Atlanta. *Sociological Spectrum* 26: 269–287.

Alba, R. D. 1992. Ethnicity. In *Encyclopedia of Sociology*, ed. E. Bargatta and M. Borgatta. New York: Macmillan.

Alba, R. D., and J. R. Logan. 1991. Variations on Two Themes: Racial and Ethnic Patterns in the Attainment of Suburban Residence. *Demography* 28: 431–453.

———. 1992. Assimilation and Stratification in the Homeownership Patterns of Racial and Ethnic Groups. *International Migration Review* 26(4): 1314–1341.

———. 1993. Minority Proximity to Whites in Suburbs: An Individual-Level Analysis of Segregation. *American Journal of Sociology* 98: 1388–1427.

Alba, R. D., J. R. Logan, and B. J. Stults. 2000. How Segregated Are Middle-Class African Americans? *Social Problems* 47: 543–558.

Alba, R. D., N. A., Denton, S. J Leung, and J. R. Logan. 1995. Neighborhood Change under Conditions of Mass Immigration: The New York City Region, 1970–1990. *International Migration Review* 29: 625–656.

Alba, R. D., J. D., Logan, B .J. Stults, G. Marzan, and W. Zhang. 1999. Immigrant Groups in the Suburbs: A Reexamination of Suburbanization and Spatial Assimilation. *American Sociological Review* 64: 446–460.

Alwin, D. F., P. E. Converse, and S. S. Martin. 1985. Living Arrangements and Social Integration. *Journal of Marriage and the Family* 47: 319–334.

Alwitt, L., and T. Donley. 1997. Retail Stores in Poor Neighborhoods. *Journal of Consumer Affairs* 31: 139–164.

Anderson, Elijah. 1990. *Streetwise: Race, Class, and Change in an Urban Community*. Chicago: University of Chicago Press.

———. 1999. *Code of the Street: Decency, Violence, and the Moral Life of the Inner-City*. New York: W. W. Norton.

Appelbaum, E., and Ronald Schettkat. 1995. Employment and Productivity in Industrialized Economies. *International Labour Review* 134: 605–623.

Ayres, I., and S. D. Levitt. 1998. Measuring Positive Externalities from Unobservable Victim Precaution: An Empirical Analysis of Lojack. *Quarterly Journal of Economics* 113 (1): 43–77.

Bailey, William C. 1984. Poverty, Inequality, and City Homicide Rates. *Criminology* 22: 531–550.

Bairoch, Paul. 1988. *Cities and Economic Development*. Chicago: University of Chicago Press.

Baller, Robert D., Luc Anselin, Steven F. Messner, Glenn Deane, and Darnell Hawkins, et al. 2001. Structural Covariates of U.S. County Homicide Rates: Incorporating Spatial Effects. *Criminology: An Interdisciplinary Journal* 39: 561–590.

Baumle, Amanda K., and Mark Fossett. 2005. Statistical Discrimination in Employment: Its Practice, Conceptualization, and Implications for Public Policy. *American Behavioral Scientist* 48: 1250–1274.

Baunach, D. M. 2002. Trends in Occupational Sex Segregation and Inequality, 1950–1990. *Social Science Research* 31 (1): 77–98.

Bean, Frank, Mark Leach, and B. Lindsay Lowell. 2004. Immigrant Job Quality and Mobility in the United States. *Work and Occupations* 31 (4): 499–518.

Beck, A. J. 2000. *Prison and Jail Inmates at Midyear 1999* (NCJ 181643). Washington, D.C.: U.S. Department of Justice, Bureau of Justice Statistics.

Behrens, A., C. Uggen, and J. Manza 2003. Ballot Manipulation and the "Menace of Negro Domination": Racial Threat and Felon Disenfranchisement in the United States, 1850–2002. *American Journal of Sociology* 109 (3): 59–605.

Belknap, Joanne. 2007. *The Invisible Woman: Gender, Crime, and Justice*. 3rd ed. Belmont, Calif.: Wadsworth/Thomson Learning.

Bellair, Paul, and Vincent J. Roscigno. 2000. Local Labor Market Opportunity and Adolescent Delinquency. *Social Forces* 78: 1509–1538.

Bellair, Paul, Vincent J. Roscigno, and Thomas L. McNulty. 2003. Linking Local Labor Market Opportunity to Violent Adolescent Delinquency. *Journal of Research in Crime and Delinquency* 40: 6–34.

Beller, Andrea H. 1984. Trends in Occupational Segregation by Sex and Race, 1960–1981. In *Sex Segregation in the Workplace*, ed. Barbara F. Reskin, 11–16. Washington, D.C.: National Academy Press.

Bingham, R., and Z. Zhang. 1997. Poverty and Economic Morphology of Ohio Central-City Neighborhoods. *Urban Affairs Review* 32: 766–796.

Blackwell, R. 1990. Parties and Factions in Trade Unions. *Employee Relations* 12 (1): 23–31.

Blalock, H. 1967. *Toward a Theory of Minority-Group Relations.* New York: Wiley.

Blau, Judith, and Peter Blau. 1982. Metropolitan Structure and Violent Crime. *American Sociological Review* 47: 114–128.

Blau, Peter. 1977. A Macrostructural Theory of Social Structure. *American Journal of Sociology* 83: 26–54.

Blauner, R. 1972. Marxian Theory and Race Relations. American Sociological Association Annual Meeting.

Bloom, Barbara, Barbara B. Owen, Jill Rosenbaum, and Elizabeth Piper Deschenes. 2003. Focusing on Girls and Young Women: A Gendered Perspective on Female Delinquency. *Women and Criminal Justice* 14: 117–136.

Blum, L., and V. Smith. 1988. Women's Mobility in the Corporation: A Critique of the Politics of Optimism. *Journal of Women in Culture and Society* 13: 528–545.

Blumer, H. 1958. Recent Research on Racial Relations: United States of America. *International Social Science Journal* 10 (3): 403–447.

Blumstein, A. 1995. Youth Violence, Guns, and the Illicit-Drug Industry. *Journal of Criminal Law and Criminology* 86 (1): 10–36.

Blumstein, A., and Richard Rosenfeld. 1998. Explaining Recent Trends in U. S. Homicide Rates. *Journal of Criminal Law and Criminology* 88 (4): 1175–1216.

Blumstein, A., F. Rivara, and R. Rosenfeld. 2000. The Rise and Decline of Homicide—And Why. *Annual Review of Public Health* 21: 505–541.

Blumstein, A., and J. Wallman. 2001. *The Crime Drop in America.* New York: Cambridge University Press.

Bobo, L., and J. Kluegel. 1997. Status, Ideology, and Dimensions of Whites' Racial Beliefs and Attitudes: Progress and Stagnation. In *Racial Attitudes in the 1990s: Continuity and Change*, ed. S. A. Tuch and J. K. Martin. Westport, Conn.: Prager.

Bobo, Lawrence, James R. Kluegel, and Ryan A. Smith. 1997. Laissez-Faire Racism: The Crystallization of a Kinder, Gentler, Anti-Black Ideology. In *Racial Attitudes in the 1990s: Continuity and Change*, ed. Steven A. Tuch and Jack K. Martin, 15–41. Westport, Conn.: Praeger.

Bobo, L., and R. Smith. 1994. Antipoverty Policy, Affirmative Action, and Racial Attitudes. In *Confronting Poverty: Prescriptions for Change*, ed. Sheldon Dezinger, Gary Sandefur, and Daniel Weinberg, 365–395. Cambridge, Mass.: Harvard University Press.

Bobo, L., and C. L. Zubrinsky. 1996. Attitudes on Residential Integration: Perceived Status Differences, Mere In-Group Preference, or Racial Prejudice? *Social Forces* 74 (3): 883–909.

Bogard, Cynthia, Alex Trillo, Michael Schwartz, and Naomi Gerstel. 2001. Future Employment among Homeless Single Mothers: The Effects of Full-Time Work Experience and Depressive Symptomatology. *Women and Health* 32: 137–157.

Bonger, Willem. 1969. *Criminality and Economic Conditions*, ed. Austin Turk. Bloomington: Indiana University Press.

Borjas, George. J. 1999. Immigration and Welfare Magnets. *Journal of Labor Economics* 17 (4): 607–637.

Borjas, George J., R. B. Freeman, and L. F. Katz. 1997. How Much Do Immigration and Trade Affects Labor Market Outcomes? *Brookings Papers on Economic Activity* 1: 1–90.

Bound, John, and Laura Dresser. 1999. The Erosion of the Relative Earnings of Young African American Women during the 1980s. In *Latinas and African American Women at Work: Race, Gender and Economic Inequality*, ed. Irene Browne. New York: Russell Sage Foundation.

Bound, John, and Harry Holzer. 1993. Industrial Shifts, Skill Levels, and the Labor Market for White and Black Males. *Review of Economics and Statistics* 75: 387–396.

Boyd, R. L. 1998. Residential Segregation by Race and the Black Merchants of Northern Cities during the Early Twentieth Century. *Sociological Forum* 13 (4): 95–609.

Box, Steven, and Chris Hale. 1983. Liberation and Female Criminality in England and Wales. *British Journal of Criminology* 23: 35–49.

Brown, M. C., and B. D. Warner. 1992. Immigrants, Urban Politics, and Policing in 1900. *American Sociological Review* 57: 293–305.

Browne, Irene. 1997. Explaining the Black-White Gap in Labor Force Participation among Women Heading Households. *American Sociological Review* 62: 236–252.

———. 2000. Opportunities Lost? Race, Industrial Restructuring and Employment among Young Women Heading Households. *Social Forces* 78 (3): 907–929.

Browne, Irene, and Rachel Askew. 2005. Race, Ethnicity, and Wage Inequality among Women: What Happened in the 1990s and Early 21st Century? *American Behavioral Scientist* 48 (9): 1275–1292.

Brunson, Rod K., and Eric A. Stewart. 2006. Young African-American Women, the Street Code, and Violence: An Exploratory Analysis. *Journal of Crime and Justice* 29 (1): 1–19.

Buckler, Kevin, and Lawrence Travis. 2003. Reanalyzing the Prevalence and Social Context of Collateral Consequence Statutes. *Journal of Criminal Justice* 31 (5): 435–453.

Bureau of Justice Statistics. 1996. *Correctional Population in the U.S., 1994.* Executive Summary. Washington, D.C.: Bureau of Justice Statistics.

————. 2001. *Prisoners in 2000.* Washington, D.C.: Bureau of Justice Statistics.

Burgess, Ernest W. 1967. The Growth of the City: An Introduction to a Research Project. In *The City,* ed. Robert Park, Ernest Burgess, and R. D. McKenzie. Chicago: University of Chicago Press.

Bursik, Robert J. 1988. Social Disorganization and Theories of Crime and Delinquency: Problems and Prospects. *Criminology* 26: 519–551.

Bursik, Robert J., Jr., and Harold Grasmick. 1993. *Neighborhoods and Crime: The Dimensions of Effective Community Control.* New York: Lexington Books.

Burtless, Gary. 1995. *The Work Alternative: Welfare Reform and the Realties of the Job Market,* ed. Demetra Smith Nightingale and Robert Haveman. Washington, D.C.: Urban Institute.

Burton, Velmer, Francis Cullen, and Lawrence Travis. 1987. The Collateral Consequences of a Felony Conviction: A National Study of State Statutes. *Federal Probation* 51: 52–60.

Byrne, James M., and Robert J. Sampson, eds. 1986. *The Social Ecology of Crime.* New York: Springer-Verlag.

Callahan, Charles, Frederick Rivera, and Thomas Koepsell. 1994. Money for Guns: Evaluation of the Seattle Gun Buy-Back Program. *Public Health Reports.* 109 (4): 472–477.

Card, David. 2005. Is the New Immigration Really So Bad? *Economic Journal* 115 (507): F300–F323.

Card, David, and J. DiNardo. 2000. Do Immigrant Inflows Lead to Native Outflows? *American Economic Review* 90 (2): 360–367.

Carlson, S. M. 1992. Trends in Race/Sex Occupational Inequality: Conceptual and Measurement Issues. *Social Problems* 39: 268–290.

Carmichael, Jason T. 2005. The Determinants of Jail Use across Large U.S. Cities: An Assessment of Racial, Ethnic, and Economic Threat Explanations. *Social Science Research* 34: 538–569.

Chamlin, Mitchell. 1989. Conflict Theory and Police Killings. *Deviant Behavior* 10 (4): 353–368.

Chambliss, W. J., and R. Seidman. 1980. *Law, Order, and Power.* Reading, Mass.: Addison-Wesley.

Charles, C. Z. 2003. The Dynamics of Racial Residential Segregation. *Annual Review of Sociology* 29: 167–207.

Chesney-Lind, Meda. 1986. Women and Crime: The Female Offender. *Signs* 12 (1): 78–96.

————. 1989. Girls' Crime and Women's Place: Toward a Feminist Model of Female Delinquency. *Crime and Delinquency* 35: 19–27.

Chiricos, Theodore. 1987. Rates of Crime and Unemployment: An Analysis of Aggregate Research Evidence. *Social Problems* 34: 187–212.

Clark, W. A. V., and S. A Blue. 2004. Race, Class, and Segregation Patterns in U.S. Immigration Gateway Cities. *Urban Affairs Review* 39: 667–688.

Clark, W. A. V., and J. Ware. 1997. Trends in Residential Integration by Socioeconomic Status in Southern California. *Urban Affairs Review* 32: 825–843.

Cohen, Lawrence, Marcus Felson, and Kenneth C. Land. 1980. Property Crime Rates in the United States: A Macro-Dynamic Analysis, 1947–1977, with ex Ante Forecasts for the Mid-1980s. *American Journal of Sociology* 86: 90–117.

Cook, Philip L., and John Laub. 1998. The Unprecedented Epidemic in Youth Violence. In *Youth, Violence, Crime, and Justice,* ed. M. Tonry and M. H. Moore, vol. 24. Chicago: University of Chicago Press.

———. 2002. After the Epidemic: Recent Trends in Youth Violence in the United States. *Crime and Justice: A Review of Research* 29: 1–37.

Cork, Daniel. 1999. Examining Space-Time Interaction in City-Level Homicide Data: Crack Markets and the Diffusion of Guns among Youth. *Journal of Quantitative Criminology* 15 (4): 379–406.

Cornell, S., and D. Hartman. 2004. Conceptual Confusion and Divides: Race, Ethnicity, and the Study of Immigration. In *Not Just Black and White: Historical and Contemporary Perspectives on Immigration, Race, and Ethnicity,* ed. N. Foner and G. M. Fredrickson, 23–41. New York: Russell Sage Foundation.

Cortes, C. E. 1980. The Chicanos—A Frontier People (Los Chicanos—Un Pueblo de Frontera). *Agenda* 10 (1): 16–21.

Corzine, J., and L. Huff-Corzine. 1992. Racial Inequality and Black Homicide: An Analysis of Felony, Nonfelony, and Total Rates. *Journal of Contemporary Criminal Justice* 8: 150–165.

Crutchfield, Robert. 1989. Labor Stratification and Violent Crime. *Social Forces* 68: 489–512.

Crutchfield, Robert, and Susan R. Pitchford. 1997. Work and Crime: The Effects of Labor Stratification. *Social Forces* 76: 93–118.

Crutchfield, Robert, Ann Glusker, and George S. Bridges. 1999. A Tale of Three Cities. *Sociological Focus* 32: 65–83.

Cullen, J. B., and S. Levitt. 1996. *Crime, Urban Flight, and the Consequences for Cities.* Cambridge, Mass.: National Bureau of Economic Research.

Daly, Kathleen, and Meda Chesney-Lind. 1988. Feminism and Criminology. *Justice Quarterly* 5: 101–143.

Datesman, S., and F. Scarpetti. 1980. Unequal Protection for Males and Females in the Juvenile Court. In *Women, Crime, and Justice,* ed. S. Datesman and F. Scarpetti, 300–319. New York: Oxford University Press.

DeFina, R. H., and T. M. Arvanites. 2002. The Weak Effect of Imprisonment on Crime: 1971–1998. *Social Science Quarterly* 83 (3): 635–653.

Devine, Joel, Joseph F. Sheley, and Dwayne M. Smith. 1998. Macroeconomic and Social-Control Policy Influences on Crime Rate Changes, 1948–1985. *American Sociological Review* 53 (3): 407–420.

DiIulio, J. J., Jr. 1995. *Broken Bottles: Liquor, Disorder, and Crime in Wisconsin.* Milwaukee, Wis.: Policy Research Institute Report 5.

Doeringer, P. B., and M. J. Piore. 1971. *Internal Labor Markets and Manpower Analysis.* Lexington, Mass.: D.C. Heath.

Duggan, Mark. 2001. More Guns, More Crime. *Journal of Political Economy* 109 (5): 1086–1114.

Eichengreen, Barry. 2004. Productivity, Growth, the New Economy, and Catching Up. *Review of International Economics* 12 (2): 243–245.

Eitle, D., S. J. D'Alessio, and L. Stolzenberg. 2006. Economic Segregation, Race, and Homicide. *Social Science Quarterly* 87 (3): 638–657.

England, Paula, Karen Christopher, and Lori Reid. 1999. Gender, Race, Ethnicity, and Wages. In *Latinas and African American Women at Work: Race, Gender, and Economic Inequality,* ed. Irene Browne, 139–182. New York: Russell Sage Foundation.

Fagan, Jeffery. 1992. Drug Selling and Licit Income in Distressed Neighborhoods: The Economic Lives of Street-level Drug Users and Sellers. In *Drugs, Crime, and Social Isolation: Barriers to Urban Opportunity,* ed. V. Harrell and G. E. Peterson, 99–146. Washington, D.C.: Urban Institute.

Farley, Reynolds. 1977. Residential Segregation in Urbanized Areas of the United States in 1970: An Analysis of Social Class and Racial Differences. *Demography* 14: 497–518.

———. 1997. Trends in Racial Inequalities—Have Gains of 1960s Disappeared in 1970s. *American Sociological Review* 42 (2): 189–208.

Farley, R., and W. R. Allen. 1989. *The Color Line and Quality of Life in America.* New York: Russell Sage Foundation.

Farley, R., S. Danziger, and H. J. Holzer. 2000. *Detroit Divided.* New York: Russell Sage Foundation.

Farley, R., and W. H. Frey. 1994. Changes in the Segregation of Whites from Blacks during the 1980s: Small Step toward a More Integrated Society. *American Sociological Review* 59 (1): 23–45.

Farley, Reynolds, Howard Schuman, Suzanne Bianchi, Diane Colasanto, and Shirley Hatchett. 1978. "'Chocolate City, Vanilla Suburbs': Will the Trend Toward Racially Separate Communities Continue?" *Social Science Research* 7: 319–344.

Feagin, Joe, and D. Eckberg. 1980. Discrimination: Motivation, Action, Effects, and Context. *Annual Review of Sociology* 6: 1–20.

Fingerhut, L. A., and J. C. Kleinman. 1989. Mortality among Children and Youth. *American Journal of Public Health* 79: 899–901.

Flewelling, Robert. 2004. A Nonparametric Imputation Approach for Dealing with Missing Variables in the SHF data. *Homicide Studies* 8: 255–266.

Fong, E., and M. Gulia. 1999. Differences in Neighborhood Qualities among Major Racial/Ethnic Groups in Canada. *Sociological Inquiry* 69: 575–598.

————. 2000. Neighborhood Change within the Canadian Ethnic Mosaic, 1986–1991. *Population Research Policy Review* 19 (2): 155–177.

Fong, E., and K. Shibuya. 2000. Suburbanization and Home Ownership: The Spatial Assimilation Process in U.S. Metropolitan Areas. *Sociological Perspectives* 43 (1): 137–157.

————. 2005. Multi-Ethnic Cities in North America. *Annual Review of Sociology* 31: 285–304.

Ford, Julie M., and Andrew A. Beveridge. 2004. "Bad" Neighborhoods, Fast Food: "Sleazy" Businesses, and Drug Dealers: Relations between the Local of Licit and Illicit Businesses in the Urban Environment. *Journal of Drug Issues* 34 (1): 51–76.

Fossett, M. A., O. R. Galle, and J. A. Burr. 1989. Racial Occupational Inequality, 1940–1980: A Research Note on the Impact of the Changing Regional Distribution of the Black Population. *Social Forces* 68: 415–427.

Fowles, Richard, and Mary Merva. 1996. Wage Inequality and Criminal Activity: An Extreme Bounds Analysis for the United States, 1975–1990. *Criminology* 34 (2): 163–182.

Fox, James A. 1997. *Trends in Juvenile Violence: An Update*. Washington D.C.: Bureau of Justice Statistics.

————. 2005. *Uniform Crime Reports [United States]: Supplementary Homicide Reports, 1976–2003*. [Computer file]. Inter-university Consortium for Political and Social Research (ICPSR) 6754.

Fredrickson, G. M. 2002. *Racism: A Short History*. Princeton, N.J.: Princeton University Press.

Freeman, Richard B., and William M. Rodgers. 1999. Area Economic Conditions and Labor Market Outcomes of Young Men in the 1990s Expansion. Cambridge, Mass.: National Bureau of Economic Research.

Frey, W. H., and R. Farley. 1996. Latino, Asian, and Black Segregation in U.S. Metropolitan Areas: Are Multiethnic Metros Different? *Demography* 33: 35–50.

Friedman, S., and G. D. Squires. 2005. Does the Community Reinvestment Act Help Minorities Access Traditionally Inaccessible Neighborhoods? *Social Problems* 52 (2): 209–231.

Gartner, Rosemary, Kathryn Baker, and Fred Pampel. 1990. Gender Stratification and the Gender Gap in Homicide Victimization. *Social Problems* 37: 593–612.

Glaeser, E. L., and D. C. Mare. 2001. Cities and Skills. *Journal of Labor Economics* 19 (2): 316–342.

Glass, Jennifer, Marta Tienda, and Shelley A. Smith. 1988. The Impact of Changing Employment Opportunity on Gender and Ethnic Earnings Inequality. *Social Science Research* 17: 252–276.

Goldin, C. S. 1990. Stigma, Biomedical Efficacy, and Institutional Control. *Social Science and Medicine* 30 (8): 895–900.

Goldstein, P. J. 1985. The Drug-Violence Nexus: A Tri-partite Conceptual Framework. *Journal of Drug Issues* 15: 493–506.

Goldstein, Paul, Henry Brownstein, Patrick Ryan, and Patricia Bellucci. 1997. Crack and Homicide in New York City: A Case Study in the Epidemiology of Violence. In *Crack in America: Demon Drugs and Social Justice*, ed. Craig Reinarmann and Harry Levine, 113–130. Berkeley: University of California Press.

Gordon, David M. 1972. *Theories of Poverty and Underemployment*. Lexington, Mass.: D.C. Health.

Gould, E. D., B. A. Weinberg, and D. B. Mustard. 2002. Crime Rates and Local Labor Market Opportunities in the United States: 1979–1997. *Review of Economics and Statistics* 84: 45–61.

Greenbaum, Robert T., and George E. Tita. 2004. The Impact of Violence Surges on Neighborhood Business Activity. *Urban Studies* 41: 2495–2514.

Greenberg, David. 1993. Delinquency and the Age Structure in Society. In *Crime and Capitalism: Readings in Marxist Criminology*, ed. David Greenberg, 334–356. Philadelphia: Temple University Press.

Greenfeld, Lawrence A., and Tracy L. Snell. 1999. *Women Offenders* (NCJ 175688). Washington, D.C.: U.S. Department of Justice, Bureau of Justice Statistics.

Grogger, Jeffrey. 2001. The Effects of Time Limits and Other Policy Changes on Welfare Use, Work, and Income among Female-Headed Families. National Bureau of Economic Research Working Paper #8153.

Grogger, Jeffrey, and Michael Willis. 2000. The Emergence of Crack Cocaine and the Rise in Urban Crime Rates. *Review of Economics and Statistics* 82: 519–529.

Hagan, John. 1994. *Crime and Disrepute*. Thousand Oaks, Calif.: Pine Forge.

Hagan, John, and Alberto Palloni. 1999. Sociological Criminology and the Mythology of Hispanic Immigration and Crime. *Social Problems* 46: 617–632.

Hagan, John, and Ruth Peterson. 1995. *Crime and Inequality*. Palo Alto, Calif.: Stanford University Press.

Hannon, L., P. Knapp, and R. DeFina. 2005. Racial Similarity in the Relationship between Poverty and Homicide Rates: Comparing Retransformed Coefficients. *Social Science Research* 34 (4): 893–914.

Harer, M. D., and Darrell Steffensmeier. 1992. The Differing Effects of Economic Inequality on Black and White Rates of Violence. *Social Forces* 70 (4): 1035–1054.

Harrison, Bennett, and Barry Bluestone. 1988. *The Great U-Turn: Corporate Restructuring and the Polarization of America*. New York: Basic Books.

Hawkins, D. F. 1987. Beyond Anomalies: Rethinking the Conflict Perspective on Race and Criminal Punishment. *Social Forces* 65: 719–745.

Hawkins, Darnell J. 1995. *Ethnicity, Race, and Crime: Perspectives across Time and Place* (SUNY Series in New Directions in Crime and Justice Studies). Albany: State University of New York Press.

Heimer, Karen. 2000. The Nature of Crime: Continuity and Change. Changes in the Gender Gap in Crime and Women's Economic Marginalization. *Criminal Justice 2000* 1: 427–483.

Hesse-Biber, S., and G. Carter. 2004. *Working Women in America: Split Dreams.* 2nd ed. New York: Oxford University Press.

Hirschman, C., A. Richard, and R. Farley. 2000. The Meaning and Measurement of Race in the U.S. Census: Glimpses into the Future. *Demography* 37 (3): 381–393.

Holloway, Steven R., and James O. Wheeler. 1991. Corporate Headquarters Relocation and Changes in Metropolitan Corporate Dominance: 1980–1987. *Economic Geography* 67: 54–74.

Holmes, Malcolm. 2000. Minority Threat and Police Brutality: Determinants of Civil Rights Criminal Complaints in U.S. Municipalities. *Criminology* 38 (2): 343–367.

Holzer, Harry. 1991. The Spatial Mismatch Hypothesis: What Has the Evidence Shown? *Urban Studies* 28: 105–122.

———. 1996. *What Employers Want: Job Prospects for Less-Educated Workers.* New York: Russell Sage Foundation.

Holzer, Harry, Paul Offner, and Elaine Sorensen. 2005. What Explains the Continuing Decline in Labor Force Activity among Young Black Men? *Labor History* 46 (1): 37–55.

Horowitz, Ruth. 1983. *Honor and the American Dream: Culture and Identity in a Chicano Community.* New Brunswick, N.J.: Rutgers University Press.

Horton, H. 1995. Population Change and the Employment Status of College-Educated Blacks. In *Research in Race and Ethnic Relations,* ed. Rutledge M. Dennis, 8. Albany: State University of New York Press.

Hsieh, Ching-Chi, and M. D. Pugh. 1993. Poverty, Income Inequality, and Violent Crime: A Meta-Analysis of Recent Aggregate Data Studies. *Criminal Justice Review* 18: 182–202.

Hsueh, S., and M. Tienda. 1996. Gender, Ethnicity, and Labor Force Instability. *Social Science Research* 25 (1): 73–94.

Iceland, J. 2004. More Pay, More Inequality? The Influence of Average Wage Levels and the Racial Composition of Jobs on the Black-White Wage Gap. *Social Science Review* 33: 498–520.

Iceland, J., D. H. Weinberg, and E. Steinmetz. 2002. *Racial and Ethnic Residential Segregation in the United States: 1980–2000. Census 2000 Special Report.* Washington, D.C.: U.S. Government Printing Office. Available at http: //www.census.gov/hhes/www/resseg.html.

Iceland, J., and R. Wilkes. 2006. Does Socioeconomic Status Matter? Race, Class, and Residential Segregation. *Social Problems* 53(2): 248–273.

Ihlanfeldt, Keith. 1992. Intraurban Wage Gradients: Evidence by Race, Gender, Occupational Class, and Sector. *Journal of Urban Economics* 32: 70–91.

Ihlanfeldt, Keith, and David Sjoquist. 1989. The Impact of Job Decentralization on the Economic Welfare of Central City Blacks. *Journal of Urban Economics* 26: 110–130.

Jackson, P., and L. Carroll. 1981. Race and the War on Crime: The Sociopolitical Determinants of Municipal Police Expenditures in 90 Non-Southern Cities. *American Sociological Review* 46: 390–405.

Jacobs, David, and Jason T. Carmichael. 2002. Subordination and Violence against State Control Agents: Testing Political Explanations for Lethal Assaults against the Police. *Social Forces* 80: 1223–1251.

Jacobsen, J. P. 1994. Sex Segregation at Work: Trends and Predictions. *Social Science Journal* 31 (2): 153–169.

Jaret, Charles, Lesley Williams Reid, and Robert M. Adelman. 2003. Black-White Income Inequality and Metropolitan Socioeconomic Structure. *Journal of Urban Affairs* 25: 305–333.

Jaynes, G. D., and R. M. Williams. 1989. *A Common Destiny: Blacks and American Society.* Washington, D.C.: National Academy Press.

Johnstone, Bob. 1999. *We Were Burning: Japanese Entrepreneurs and the Forging of the Electronic Age.* New York: Basic Books.

Jones, J. A., and R. A. Rosenfeld. 1989. Women's Occupations and Local Labor Markets: 1950 to 1980. *Social Forces* 67: 666–692.

Jorgenson, Dale W. 2001. Information Technology and the U.S. Economy. *American Economic Review* 91 (1): 1–32.

Kain, J. 1992. The Spatial Mismatch Hypothesis: The Decades Later. *Housing Policy Debate* 3: 175–197.

Kaker, Suman, Marie-Louise Friedmann, and Linda Peck. 2002. Girls in Detention: The Results of Focus Group Discussion Interviews and Official Records Review. *Journal of Contemporary Criminal Justice* 18: 57–73.

Kasarda, John D. 1983. Entry-Level Jobs, Mobility, and Urban Minority Unemployment. *Urban Affairs Quarterly* 19: 21–40.

———. 1989. Urban Industrial Transition and the Underclass. *Annuals of the American Academy of Political and Social Science* 501: 26–47.

———. 1992. The Severely Distressed in Economically Transforming Cities. In *Drugs, Crime, and Social Isolation: Barriers to Urban Opportunity,* ed. Adele V. Harrell and George E. Peterson, 45–97. Washington, D.C.: The Urban Institute.

———. 1995. Industrial Restructuring and the Changing Location of Jobs. In *State of the Union: America in the 1990s,* ed. Reynolds Farley, 215–267. New York: Russell Sage Foundation.

Katz, Lawrence, and Kevin M. Murphy. 1992. Changes in Relative Wages, 1965–1987: Supply and Demand Factors. *Quarterly Journal of Economics* 107: 35–78.

Kaufman, R. L. 1986. The Impact of Industrial and Occupational Structure on Black-White Employment Allocation. *American Sociological Review* 51 (3): 310–323.

Kellam, S. G., R. G. Adams, C. H. Brown, and M. E. Ensminger. 1982. The Long-Term Evolution of the Family Structure of Teenage and Older Mothers. *Journal of Marriage and the Family* 44: 539–554.

Kennelly, Ivy. 1999. "That Single Mother Element": How White Employers Typify Black Women. *Gender and Society* 13: 168–193.

Kessler, Daniel, and Steven Levitt. 1999. Using Sentence Enhancements to Distinguish between Deterrence and Incapacitation. *Journal of Law and Economics* 42: 343–363.

King. M. C. 1992. Occupational Segregation by Race and Sex: 1940–1988. *Monthly Labor Review* (April): 30–37.

Kirschenman, Joleen, and Kathryn Neckerman. 1991. "We'd Love to Hire Them, but . . ." The Meaning of Race for Employers. In *The Urban Underclass*, ed. Christopher Jencks and Paul Peterson, 203–234. Washington, D.C.: Brookings Institution.

Klein, D., and J. Kress. 1976. Any Woman's Blues: A Critical Overview of Women, Crime, and the Criminal Justice System. *Crime and Social Justice* 5: 34–49.

Kletzer, Lori. 1991. Job Displacement, 1979–1986: How Blacks Fared Relative to Whites. *Monthly Labor Review* (July): 17–25.

Kluegel, J. R. 1999. An American Dilemma Revisited: Race Relations in a Changing World. *Social Forces* 77 (3): 1207–1209.

Koons-Witt, Barbara A., and Pamela J. Schram. 2003. The Prevalence and Nature of Violent Offending by Females. *Journal of Criminal Justice* 31: 361–371.

Krivo, L., and R. L. Kaufman. 1999. How Low Can It Go? Declining Black-White Segregation in a Multiethnic Context. *Crime and Social Justice* 5: 34–49.

Krivo, Lauren, and Ruth D. Peterson. 1996. Extremely Disadvantaged Neighborhoods and Urban Crime. *Social Forces* 75: 619–648.

———. 2000. The Structural Context of Homicide: Accounting for Racial Differences in Process. *American Sociological Review* 65 (4): 547–559.

———. 2004. Labor Market Conditions and Violent Crime among Youth and Adults. *Sociological Perspectives* 47 (4): 485–505.

Kubrin, Charis E., and Ronald Weitzer. 2003. Retaliatory Homicide: Concentrated Disadvantage and Neighborhood Culture. *Social Problems* 50: 157–180.

Kuziemko, Ilyana, and Steven Levitt. 2003. An Empirical Analysis of Imprisoning Drug Offenders. *Journal of Public Economics* 88 (9–10): 2043–2066.

LaFree, Gary. 1999. Declining Violent Crime Rates in the 1990s: Predicting Crime Booms and Busts. *Annual Review of Sociology* 25: 145–168.

LaFree, G., and K. A. Drass. 1996. The Effect of Changes in Intraracial Income Inequality and Educational Attainment on Changes in Arrest Rates for African Americans and Whites, 1957 to 1990. *American Sociological Review* 61 (4): 614–634.

LaFree, G., K. Drass, and P. O'Day. 1992. Race and Crime in Postwar America: Determinants of African-American and White Rates, 1957–1988. *American Sociological Review* 61 (4): 614–640.

LaFree, G., Robert O'Brien, and Eric Baumer. 2006. Is the Gap between Black and White Arrest Rates Narrowing? National Trends for Personal Contact Crimes, 1960 to 2002. In *The Many Colors of Crime: Inequalities of Race, Ethnicity, and Crime in America*, ed. Ruth Peterson, Lauren Krivo, and John Hagan. New York: New York University Press.

Land, Kenneth C., Patricia L. McCall, and Lawrence E. Cohen. 1990. Structural Covariates of Homicide Rates: Are There Any Invariances Across Time and Social Space? *American Journal of Sociology* 95: 922–963.

Laub, J., and R. J. Sampson. 1993. Turning Points in the Life Course: Why Change Matters to the Study of Crime. *Criminology* 31 (3): 301–325.

Lee, Matthew R. 2000. Concentrated Poverty, Race, and Homicide. *Sociological Quarterly* 41 (2): 189–206.

Lee, Matthew R., and Graham C. Ousey. 2005. Institutional Access, Residential Segregation, and Urban Black Homicide. *Sociological Inquiry* 75 (1): 31–54.

Levin, J., and W. Levin. 1982. *The Functions of Discrimination and Prejudice.* 2nd ed. New York: Harper and Row.

Levitt, Steven D. 2001. Alternative Strategies for Identifying the Link between Unemployment and Crime. *Journal of Quantitative Criminology* 17: 377–390.

———. 2004. Understanding Why Crime Fell in the 1990s: Four Factors That Explain the Decline and Six That Do Not. *Journal of Economic Perspectives* 18 (1): 163–190.

Lian, B., and J. R. Oneal. 1997. Cultural Diversity and Economic Development: A Cross-National of 98 Countries, 1960–1985. *Economic Development and Cultural Change* 46 (1): 61–77.

Lieberson, S. 1980. *A Piece of the Pie: Black and White Immigration since 1880.* Berkeley: University of California Press.

Light, I. H., and E. Bonacich. 1988. *Immigrant Entrepreneurs: Koreans in Los Angeles, 1965–1982.* Berkeley: University of California Press.

Liska, A. E., and M. B. Chamlin. 1984. Social Structure and Crime Control among Macrosocial Units. *American Journal of Sociology* 90: 383–395.

Liska, Allen E., Joseph J. Lawrence, and Michael Benson. 1981. Perspectives on the Legal Order: The Capacity for Social Control. *American Journal of Sociology* 87: 413–26.

Loftin, Colin, David McDowall, Brian Wiersema, and Talbert Cottey. 1991. Effects of restrictive licensing of handguns on homicide and suicide in the District of Columbia. *New England Journal of Medicine* 325 (23): 1615–1620.

Logan, J., R. Alba, and W. Zhang. 2002. Immigrant Enclaves and Ethnic Communities in New York and Los Angeles. *American Sociological Review* 67 (2): 299–322.

Logan, J. R., and Steven F. Messner. 1987. Racial Residential Segregation and Suburban Violent Crime. *Social Science Quarterly* 68 (3): 510–527.

Logan, J. R., B. J. Stults, and R. Farley. 2004. Segregation of Minorities in the Metropolis: Two Decades of Change. *Demography* 41: 1–22.

Lott, John R., and David B. Mustard. 1997. Crime, Deterrence, and Right-to-Carry Concealed Handguns. *Journal of Legal Studies* 26: 1–68.

Loury, G. C. 2002. *The Anatomy of Racial Inequality.* Cambridge, Mass.: Harvard University Press.

Ludwig, Jens, and Philip Cook. 2000. Homicide and Suicide Rates Associated with Implementation of the Brady Handgun Violence Prevention Act. *Journal of the American Medical Association* 284 (5): 585–591.

Lynch, J., and W. Sabol. 1997. *Did Getting Tough on Crime Pay?* Washington, D.C.: Urban Institute.

Maher, Lisa. 1997. *Sexed Work: Gender, Race, and Resistance in a Brooklyn Drug Market.* Clarendon Studies in Criminology. Oxford: Oxford University Press.

Maltz, M. D. 1998. Which Homicides Decreased? Why? *Journal of Criminal Law and Criminology* 88: 1489–1496.

Mann, Catherine. 2004. The U.S. Current Account, New Economy Services, and Implications for Sustainability. *Review of International Economics* 12 (2): 262–276.

Marcuse, P. 1997. The Enclave, the Citadel, and the Ghetto: What Has Changed in the Post-Fordist U.S. City. *Urban Affairs Review* 33 (2): 228–264.

Martinez, Ramiro, Jr. 2002. *Latino Homicide: Immigration, Violence, and Community.* New York: Routledge.

Marvell, Thomas, and Carlisle Moody. 1994. Prison Population Growth and Crime Reduction. *Journal of Quantitative Criminology* 10 (2): 109–140.

———. 1996. Determinants Sentencing and Abolishing Parole: The Long-Term Impacts on Prison and Crime. *Criminology* 34: 257–267.

———. 1997. The Impact of Prison Growth on Homicide. *Homicide Studies* 1: 205–233.

Massey, D. S. 1990. American Apartheid: Segregation and the Making of the Underclass. *American Journal of Sociology* 96: 329–357.

———. 1999. International Migration at the Dawn of the Twenty-First Century: The Role of the State. *Population and Development Review* 25 (2): 303–322.

Massey, D. S., and N. A. Denton. 1988. Suburbanization and Segregation in United States Metropolitan Areas. *American Sociological Review* 94: 592–626.

———. 1993. *American Apartheid: Segregation and the Making of the Underclass.* Cambridge, Mass.: Harvard University Press.

Massey, Douglas S., and Mitchell L. Eggers. 1990. The Ecology of Inequality: Minorities and the Concentration of Poverty, 1970–1980. *American Journal of Sociology* 95: 1153–1188.

Massey, D. S., and E. Fong. 1990. Segregation and Neighborhood Quality: Blacks, Hispanics, and Asians in the San Francisco Metropolitan Area. *Social Forces* 69: 15–32.

Massey, Douglas S., Andrew B. Gross, and Mitchell L. Eggers. 1991. Segregation, the Concentration of Poverty, and the Life Chances of Individuals. *Social Science Research* 20: 397–420.

Massey, Douglas S., Andrew B. Gross, and Kumiko Shibuya. 1994. Migration, Segregation, and the Geographic Concentration of Poverty. *American Sociological Review* 59: 425–445.

Massey, D.S., and B. P. Mullan. 1984. Processes of Hispanic and Black Spatial Assimilation. *American Journal of Sociology* 89 (4): 836–873.

Mauer, Marc. 1999. *Race to Incarcerate.* New York: New Press/Norton.

———. 2003. *Comparative International Rates of Incarceration: An Examination of Causes and Trends.* Presented to the U.S. Commission on Civil Rights. Available at www.sentencingproject.com.

McCall, Leslie. 2000. Explaining Levels of Within-Group Wage Inequality in U.S. Labor Markets. *Demography* 37 (4): 415–430.

———. 2001. *Complex Inequality: Gender, Class, and Race in the New Economy.* New York: Routledge.

McNulty, T. L. 2001. Assessing the Race-Violence Relationship at the Macro Level: The Assumption of Racial Invariance and the Problem of Restricted Distributions. *Criminology* 39 (2): 467–490.

Merton, Robert. 1938. Social Structure and Anomie. *American Sociological Review* 3: 672–682.

———. 1947. Selected Problems of Field Work in the Planned Community. *American Sociological Review* 12 (3): 304–312.

———. 1968. *Social Theory and Social Structure.* New York: Free Press.

Messerschmidt, James W. 1986. *Capitalism, Patriarchy, and Crime: Toward a Socialist Feminist Criminology.* Totowa, N.J.: Rowman and Littlefield.

———. 1988. From Marx to Bonger: Socialist Writings on Women, Gender, and Crime. *Sociological Inquiry* 58 (4): 378–392.

Messner, Steven. 1982. Poverty, Inequality, and the Urban Homicide Rate. *Criminology* 20: 103–115.

———. 1989. Economic Discrimination and Societal Homicide Rates: Further Evidence of the Cost of Inequality. *American Sociological Review* 54: 597–611.

Messner, Steven, Glenn Deane, Luc Anselin, and Benjamin Pearson-Nelson. 2005. Locating the Vanguard in Rising and Falling Homicide Rates across U.S. Cities. *Criminology* 43 (3): 661–696.

Messner, Steven F., Glenn Deane, and Mark Beaulieu. 2002. A Log-Multiplicative Association Model for Allocating Homicides with Unknown Victim-Offender Relationships. *Criminology* 40 (2): 457–479.

Messner, Steven, and Reid Golden. 1992. "Racial Inequality and Racially Disaggregated Homicide Rates: An Assessment of Alternative Theoretical Explanations." *Criminology* 30 (3): 421–448.

Messner, Steven, L. Raffalovich, and R. McMillan. 2001. Economic Deprivation and Changes in Homicide Arrest Rates for White and Black Youths, 1967–1998: A National Time-Series Analysis. *Criminology* 39 (3): 591–614.

Messner, Steven, and Richard Rosenfeld. 2001. *Crime and the American Dream.* Belmont, Calif.: Wadsworth.

Messner, Steven F., and R. J. Sampson. 1991. The Sex Ratio, Family Disruption, and Rates of Violent Crime: The Paradox of Demographic Structure. *Social Forces* 69 (3): 693–713.

Messner, Steven, and K. Tardiff. 1986. Economic Inequality and Levels of Homicide: An Analysis of Urban Neighborhoods. *Criminology* 24 (2): 297–317.

Min, Pyong Gap. 1996. *Caught in the Middle: Korean Communities in New York and Los Angeles.* Berkeley: University of California Press.

Morenoff, Jeffrey D., Robert J. Sampson, and Stephen W. Raudenbush. 2001. Neighborhood Inequality, Collective Efficacy, and the Spatial Dynamics of Urban Violence. *Criminology* 39: 517–558.

Moss, Philip, and Chris Tilly. 1996. Soft-Skills and Race: An Investigation of Black Men's Employment Problems. *Work and Occupations* 23: 252–276.

Myers, M. A. 1990. Economic Threat and Racial Disparities in Incarceration: The Case of Postbellum Georgia. *Criminology* 28 (4): 627–656.

National Research Council. 2004. *Measuring Racial Discrimination: Panel of Methods for Assessing Discrimination.* Edited by Rebecca M Blank, Marilyn Dababy, and Constance Citcro. Washington, D.C.: National Academy Press.

Nee, V., and J. Sanders. 2001. Understanding the Diversity of Immigrant Incorporation: A Forms-of-Capital Model. *Ethnic and Racial Studies* 24 (3): 386–411.

Nelson, Joel, and Jon Lorence. 1988. Metropolitan Earnings Inequality and Service Sector Employment. *Social Forces* 67: 492–511.

Offner, Paul, and H. Holzer. 2002. Forgotten Men: The Continuing Crisis in Black Male Unemployment, and How to Remedy It. *The American Prospect* 13 (13).

Oliner, S. D., and D. E. Sichel. 2000. The Resurgence of Growth in the Late 1990s: Is Information Technology the Story? *Journal of Economic Perspectives* 14 (4): 3–22.

Olivares, K. M., V. S. Burton, and F. T. Cullen. 1996. The Collateral Consequences of a Felony Conviction: A National Study of State Legal Codes 10 Years Later. *Federal Probation* 60 (3): 10–17.

Ondrich, Jan, Stephen Ross, and John Yinger. 2000. How Common Is Housing Discrimination? Improving on Traditional Measures. *Journal of Urban Economics* 47: 470–500.

———. 2003. Now You See It, Now You Don't: Why do Real Estate Agents Withhold Available Houses from Black Customers? *Review of Economics and Statistics* 85: 854–873.

Ottaviano, G. I. P., and G. Peri. 2005. Cities and Cultures. *Journal of Urban Affairs.* 58 (2): 304–337.

Ousey, Graham. 1999. Homicide, Structural Factors, and the Racial Invariance Assumption. *Criminology* 37: 405–426.

Ousey, Graham, and Matthew Lee. 2002. Examining the Conditional Nature of Illicit Drug Market-Homicide Relationship: A Partial Test of the Theory of Contingent Causation. *Criminology* 40: 73–102.

———. 2004. Investigating the Connections between Race, Illicit Drug Markets, and Lethal Violence, 1984–1997. *Journal of Research in Crime and Delinquency* 41 (4): 352–383.

Packer, Arnold, and John G. Wirt. 1992. Changing Skills in the U.S. Workforce: Trends of Supply and Demand. In *Urban Labor Markers and Job Opportunity*, ed. George E. Peterson and Wayne Vroman. Washington, D.C.: Urban Institute.

Park, Kyeyoung. 1997. *The Korean American Dream: Immigrants and Small Business in New York City*. Ithaca, N.Y.: Cornell University Press.

Parker, Karen F. 2001. A Move toward Specificity: Examining Urban Disadvantage and Race—and Relationship—Specific Homicide Rates. *Journal of Quantitative Criminology* 17 (1): 89–110.

———. 2004. Polarized Labor Market, Industrial Restructuring and Urban Violence: A Dynamic Model of the Economic Transformation Urban Violence. *Criminology* 42: 619–645.

Parker, Karen F., and Tracy Johns. 2002. Urban Disadvantage and Types of Race-Specific Homicide: Assessing the Diversity in Family Structures in the Urban Context. *Journal of Research in Crime and Delinquency* 39 (3): 277–303.

Parker, Karen F., John MacDonald, and Wesley Jennings. 2005. Racial Threat, Urban Conditions, and Police Use of Force: Assessing the Direct and Indirect Linkages across Multiple Urban Areas. *Justice Research and Policy* 7 (1): 53–79.

Parker, Karen F., and Scott Maggard. 2005. Structural Theories and Race-Specific Drug Arrests: What Structural Factors Account for the Rise in Race-Specific Drug Arrests over Time? *Crime and Delinquency* 51 (4): 521–547.

Parker, Karen F., and Patricia L. McCall. 1997. Adding Another Piece to the Inequality-Homicide Puzzle: The Impact of Structural Inequality on Racially Disaggregated Homicide Rates. *Homicide Studies* 1: 35–60.

———. 1999. Structural Conditions and Racial Homicide Patterns: A look at the Multiple Disadvantages in Urban Areas. *Criminology* 37 (3): 447–473.

Parker, Karen F., Patricia L. McCall, and Kenneth C. Land. 1999. Determining Social-Structural Predictors of Homicide: Units of Analysis and Related Methodological Concerns. In *Homicide: A Sourcebook of Social Research*, ed. M. Dwayne Smith and Margaret A. Zahn, 107–124. Thousand Oaks, Calif.: Sage.

Parker, Karen F., Brian Stults, and Stephen Rice. 2005. Racial Threat, Concentrated Disadvantage, and Social Control: Considering the Macro-Level Sources of Variation in Arrests. *Criminology* 43 (4): 1111–1134.

Parker, Karen F., and Matthew V. Pruitt. 2000a. How the West Was One: Explaining the Similarities in Race-Specific Homicide Rates in the West and South. *Social Forces* 78 (4): 1483–1508.

———. 2000b. Poverty, Poverty Concentration, and Homicide. *Social Science Quarterly* 81 (2): 555–570.

Patterson, E. Britt. 1991. Poverty, Income Inequality, and Community Crime Rates. *Criminology* 29: 755–776.

Petee, T. A., and G. S. Kowalski. 1993. Modeling Rural Violent Crime Rates: A Test of Social Disorganization Theory. *Sociological Focus* 26: 87–89.

Peterson, Ruth, and William C. Bailey 1988. Forcible Rape, Poverty and Economic Inequality in U.S. Metropolitan Communities. *Journal of Quantitative Criminology* 4: 99–119.

Peterson, Ruth, and Laura Krivo. 1993. Racial Segregation and Black Urban Homicide. *Social Forces* 71: 1001–1026.

———. 1999. Racial Segregation, the Concentration of Disadvantage, and Black and White Homicide Victimization. *Sociological Forum* 14 (3): 465–493.

Pettigrew, Thomas F. 1979. The Ultimate Attribution Error: Extending Allport's Cognitive Analysis of Prejudice. *Personality and Social Psychology Bulletin* 5: 460–476.

Phillips, Anne. 1987. *Divided Loyalties: Dilemmas of Sex and Class*. London: Virago.

Phillips, Julie. 1997. Variation in African American Homicide Rates: An Assessment of Potential Explanations. *Criminology* 35 (4): 527–560.

———. 2002. White, Black, and Latino Homicide Rates: Why the Difference? *Social Problems* 49 (3): 349–374.

Portes, Alejandro, and Rueben Rumbaut. 1996. *Immigrant America: A Portrait.* Berkeley: University of California Press.

Pratt, Travis. 2002. Meta-Analysis and Its Discontents: Treatment Destruction Techniques Revisited. *Journal of Offender Rehabilitation* 35: 23–40.

Pratt, Travis C., and Francis T. Cullen. 2005. Assessing Macro-level Predictors and Theories of Crime: a Meta-Analysis. *Crime and Justice: A Review of Research* 32: 373–450.

Pridemore, W. A. 2002. What We Know about Social Structure and Homicide: A Review of the Theoretical and Empirical Literature. *Violence and Victims* 17 (2): 127–156.

Quigley, J. M. 1998. Urban Diversity and Economic Growth. *Journal of Economic Perspectives* 12 (2): 127–138.

Quinney, Richard. 1974. *Critique of Legal Order: Crime Control in Capitalist Society.* Boston: Little, Brown.

———. 1975. *Criminology: Analysis and Critique of Crime in America.* Boston: Little, Brown.

———. 1980. *Class, State, and Crime.* 2nd ed. New York: Longman.

Raphael, Stephen, and Jens Ludwig. 2003. Prison Sentence Enhancements: The Case of Project Exile. In *Evaluating Gun Policy: Effects on Crime and Violence*, ed. Jens Ludwig and Philip Cook, 251–286. Washington, D.C: Brookings Institution.

Reid, L. W., and B. A. Rubin. 2003. Integrating Economic Dualism and Labor Market Segmentation: The Effects of Race, Gender, and Structural Location on Earnings, 1974–2000. *Sociological Quarterly* 44 (3): 405–432.

Reiman, Jeffrey. 1984. *The Rich Get Richer and the Poor Get Prison: Ideology, Class, and Criminal Justice.* 2nd ed. New York: Wiley.

Reuter, Peter, and Jenny Mouzos. 2003. Australia: A Massive Buyback of Low-Risk Guns. In *Evaluating Gun Policy: Effects of Crime and Violence*, ed. Jens Ludwig and Philip Cook, 121–156. Washington, D.C.: Brookings Institution.

Ricketts, E., and I. Sawhill. 1988. Defining and Measuring the Underclass. *Journal of Policy Analysis and Management* 7: 316–325.

Rose, Dina, and Todd Clear. 1998. Incarceration, Social Capital, and Crime: Implications for Social Disorganization Theory. *Criminology* 36: 441–479.

Rosenbaum, E., and S. Friedman. 2001. Differences in the Locational Attainment of Immigrant and Native-Born Households with Children in New York City. *Demography* 38 (3): 337–348.

Rosenfeld, M. J., and M. Tienda. 1999. Mexican Immigration, Occupational Niches, and Labor Market Competition: Evidence from Los Angeles, Chicago, and Atlanta: 1970–1990. In *Immigration and Opportunity: Race, Ethnicity, and Employment in the United States*, ed. F. Bean and S. Bell-Rose, 64–105. New York: Russell Sage.

Rosenfeld, Richard. 1996. Gun Buy-Backs: Crime Control or Community Mobilization. In *Under Fire: Gun Buy-Backs, Exchanges, and Amnesty Programs*, ed. Martha Plotkin, 1–28. Washington, D.C.: Police Executive Research Forum.

Rosenfeld, Richard, and Scott H. Decker. 1999. Are Arrest Statistics a Valid Measure of Illicit Drug Use? The Relationship between Criminal Justice and Public Health Indicators of Cocaine, Heroin, and Marijuana Use. *Justice Quarterly* 16 (3): 685–699.

Ross, S., and M. Turner. 2005. Housing Discrimination in Metropolitan America: Explaining Changes between 1989 and 2000. *Social Problems* 52 (2): 152–180.

Runciman, W. G. 1966. *Relative Deprivation and Social Justice: A Study of Attitudes to Social Inequality in Twentieth-Century England*. London: Routledge and Kegan Paul.

Sampson, Robert J. 1985. Neighborhood and Crime—The Structural Determinants of Personal Victimization. *Journal of Research in Crime and Delinquency* 22 (1): 7–40.

———. 1986. Crime in Cities: The Effects of Formal and Informal Social Control. In *Crime and Justice,* ed. Albert Reiss and Michael Tonry, 8: 271–311. Chicago: University of Chicago Press.

———. 1987. Urban Back Violence: The Effect of Male Joblessness and Family Disruption. *American Journal of Sociology* 93 (2): 348–382.

———. 2002. Transcending Tradition: New Directions in Community Research, Chicago Style. *Criminology* 40 (2): 213–230.

Sampson, Robert J., and Lydia Bean. 2006. Cultural Mechanisms and Killing Fields: A Revised Theory of Community-Level Racial Inequality. In *The Many Colors of Crime: Inequalities of Race, Ethnicity and Crime in America*, ed. Ruth Peterson, Lauren Krivo, and John Hagan. New York: New York University Press.

Sampson, Robert J., and W. Byron Groves. 1989. Community Structure and Crime: Testing Social-Disorganization Theory. *American Journal of Sociology* 94: 774–802.

Sampson, Robert J., and Janet L. Lauritsen. 1997. Racial and Ethnic Disparities in Crime and Criminal Justice in the United States. In *Crime and Justice: A Review of Research*, ed. Michael Tonry, 21: 311–374. Special volume: *Ethnicity, Crime, and Immigration: Comparative and Cross-National Perspectives.* Chicago: University of Chicago Press.

Sampson Robert J., Jeffrey Morenoff, and Felton Earls. 1999. Beyond Social Capital: Spatial Dynamics of Collective Efficacy for Children. *American Sociological Review* 64: 633–660.

Sampson, Robert, Jeffrey Morenoff, and Stephen Raudenbush. 2005. Social Anatomy of Racial and Ethnic Disparities in Violence. *American Journal of Public Health* 95 (2): 224–232.

Sampson, Robert J., Stephen W. Raudenbush, and Felton Earls. 1997. Neighborhoods and Violent Crime: A Multilevel Study of Collective Efficacy. *Science* 227: 916–924.

Sampson, Robert J., and William Julius Wilson. 1995. Toward a Theory of Race, Crime, and Urban Inequality. In *Crime and Inequality*, ed. John Hagan and Ruth Peterson, 37–56. Stanford, Calif.: Stanford University Press.

Sassen, S. 1994. The Urban Complex in a World Economy. *International Social Science Journal* 46 (1): 43–62.

Schwartzman, D. 1997. Black Male Unemployment. *Review of Black Political Economy* 25: 78–93.

Seibert, M. Therese, Mark A. Fossett, and Dawn M. Baunach. 1997. Trends in Male-Female Status Inequality: 1940–1990. *Social Science Research* 26: 1–24.

Shaw, Clifford R., and Henry D. McKay. 1942. *Juvenile Delinquency and Urban Areas: A Study of Rates of Delinquents in Relation to Differential Characteristics of Local Communities in American Cities*. Chicago: University of Chicago Press.

Shepard, E. M., and P. R. Blackley. 2005. Drug Enforcement and Crime: Recent Evidence from New York State. *Social Science Quarterly* 2: 323–342.

Shihadeh, Edward S., and Nicole Flynn. 1996. Segregation and Crime: The Effect of Black Isolation on the Rates of Black Urban Violence. *Social Forces* 74 (4): 1325–1352.

Shihadeh, Edward, and M. Maume. 1997. Segregation and Crime: The Relationship between Black Centralization and Urban Black Homicide. *Homicide Studies* 1 (3): 254–280.

Shihadeh, Edward S., and Graham C. Ousey. 1996. Metropolitan Expansion and Black Social Dislocation: The Link between Suburbanization and Center-City Crime. *Social Forces* 75 (2): 649–666.

———. 1998. Industrial Restructuring and Violence: The Link between Entry-Level Jobs, Economic Deprivation, and Black and White Homicide. *Social Forces* 77 (1): 185–206.

Shihadeh, Edward S., and Darrell J. Steffensmeier. 1994. The Effects of Economic Inequality and Family Disruption on Urban Black Violence: Cities as Units of Stratification and Social Control. *Social Forces* 73: 729–751.

Short, James. 1997. *Poverty, Ethnicity, and Violent Crime*. Boulder, Colo.: Westview.

Smith, D. A., and G. A. Jarjoura. 1988. Social Structure and Criminal Victimization. *Journal of Research in Crime and Delinquency* 25: 27–52.

Smith, M. D. 1992. Variation in Correlates of Race-Specific Urban Homicide Rates. *Journal of Contemporary Criminal Justice* 8: 137–149.

Smith, M .D., and V. E. Brewer. 1992. Sex-Specific Analysis of Correlates of Homicide Victimization in United State Cities. *Violence and Victims* 7 (4): 279–286.

Sokoloff, Natalie. 1992. *Black and White Women in the Professions.* New York: Routledge.

Steffensmeier, Darrell, and Emilie Allan. 1996. Gender and Crime: Toward a Gendered Theory of Female Offending. *Annual Review of Sociology* 22: 459–487.

Steffensmeier, Darrell, and Dana Haynie. 2000. Gender, Structural Disadvantage, and Urban Crime: Do Macrosocial Variables also Explain Female Offending Rates? *Criminology* 38: 403–438.

Steinberg, R. 1997. Overall Evaluation of Economic Theories. *Voluntas* 8 (2): 179–204.

Taylor, Ian. 1999. *Crime in Context: A Critical Criminology of Market Societies.* Boulder, Colo.: Westview.

Taylor, Marylee C. 1998. How White Attitudes Vary with the Racial Composition of Local Populations: Numbers Count. *American Sociological Review* 63: 512–535.

Thompson, M. A. 2000. Black-White Residential Segregation in Atlanta. In *The Atlanta Paradox,* ed. D. L. Sjoquist, 88–115. New York: Russell Sage Foundation.

Tienda, Marta. 1989. Race, Ethnicity and the Portrait of Inequality: Approaching the 1990s. *Sociological Spectrum* 9 (1): 23–52.

Tienda, Marta, and D. T. Lii. 1987. Minority Concentration and Earnings Inequality: Blacks, Hispanics, and Asians Compared. *American Journal of Sociology* 93: 141–165.

Tienda, Marta, Shelley Smith, and Vilma Ortiz. 1987. Industrial Restructuring, Gender Segregation, and Sex Differences in Earnings. *American Sociological Review* 52: 195–210.

Tittle, Charles, R. 1983. Social Class and Criminal Behavior: A Critique of the Theoretical Foundation. *Social Forces* 62 (2): 334–358.

Tomaskovic-Devey, Donald, M. Mason, and M. Zingraff. 2004. Looking for the Driving while Black Phenomena: Conceptualizing Racial Bias Processes and Their Associated Distributions. *Police Quarterly* 7 (1): 3–29.

Tomaskovic-Devey, D., and V. Roscigno. 1996. Racial Economic Subordination and White Gain in the U.S. South. *American Sociological Review* 61: 565–589.

Tonry, Michael. 1995. *Malign Neglect.* New York: Oxford University Press.

Turk, Austin. 1966. Conflict and Criminality. *American Sociological Review* 31: 338–352.

Uggen, C., and J. Janikula. 1999. Volunteerism and Arrest in the Transition to Adulthood. *Social Forces* 78 (1): 331–362.

Uggen, C., and J. Manza. 2002. Democratic Contraction? Political Consequences of Felon Disenfranchisement in the United States. *American Sociological Review* 67: 777–803.

U.S. Census Bureau. 2005. American Community Survey.

U.S. Department of Commerce. 1993. *1992 AFDC Recipient Characteristics Study*. Administration for children and families, office of family assistance. Government Printing Office.

U.S. Department of Justice. 2003. *Prevalence of Imprisonment in the U.S. Population, 1974–2001*. NCJ 197976 Special Report of the Office of Justice Programs.

U.S. Department of Labor, Bureau of Labor Statistics. 2002. "Characteristics of Minimum Wage Workers: 2002."

Wacquant, Loic. 2000. The New Particular Institution: On the Prison as Surrogate Ghetto. *Theoretical Criminology* 4: 377–389.

Wadsworth, Tim. 2000. Labor Markets, Delinquency, and Social Control Theory: An Empirical Assessment of the Mediating Process. *Social Forces* 78: 1041–1066.

Wadsworth, Tim, and Charis Kubrin. 2004. "Structural Factors and Black Interracial Homicide: A New Examination of the Causal Process." *Criminology* 42 (3): 647–672.

Waldinger, R. D. 1996. *Still the Promised City?: African Americans and New Immigrants in Post-Industrial New York*. Cambridge, Mass.: Harvard University Press.

Walker, Samuel, Cassia Spohn, and Miriam Delone. 2003. *The Color of Justice: Race, Ethnicity, and Crime in America*. 3rd ed. Belmont, Calif.: Wadsworth.

Warner, Barbara D. 2003. The Role of Attenuated Culture in Social Disorganization Theory. *Criminology* 41 (1): 73–98.

Weiss, Harold E., and Lesley Williams Reid. 2005. Low-Quality Employment Concentration and Crime: An Examination of Metropolitan Labor Markets. *Sociological Perspectives* 48 (2): 213–232.

Wells, W., J. A. Schafer, and S. P. Varano. 2006. Neighborhood Residents' Production of Order: The Effects of Collective Efficacy on Responses to Neighborhood Problems. *Crime and Delinquency* 52 (4): 523–550.

Western, Bruce, and Becky Pettit. 2000. Incarceration and Racial Inequality in Men's Employment. *Industrial and Labor Relations Review* 54: 3–16.

———. 2002. Beyond Crime and Punishment: Prisons and Inequality. *Contexts* 1: 37–43.

———. 2005. Black-White Wage Inequality, Employment Rates, and Incarceration. *American Journal of Sociology* 111: 553–578.

Wheelock, Darren. 2005. Collateral Consequences and Racial Inequality. *Journal of Contemporary Criminal Justice* 21 (1): 82–90.

White, M. J., E. Fong, and Q. Cai. 2003. The Segregation of Asian-Origin Groups in the United States and Canada. *Social Science Research* 32: 148–167.

Wilcox, Pamela, N. Quisenberry, and D. T. Cabrera. 2004. Busy Places and Broken Windows? Toward Defining the Role of Physical Structure and Process in Community Crime Models. *Sociological Quarterly* 45 (2): 185–207.

Williams, Kirk, and Robert L. Flewelling. 1987. Family, Acquaintance, and Stranger Homicide: Alternative Procedures for Rate Calculations. *Criminology* 25: 543–560.

———. 1988. The Social Production of Criminal Homicide: A Comparative Study of Disaggregated Rates in U.S. Cities. *American Sociological Review* 53: 421–431.

Wilson, William Julius. 1987. *The Truly Disadvantaged: The Inner City, the Underclass, and Public Policy.* Chicago: University of Chicago Press.

———. 1991. Studying Inner-city Social Dislocations: The Challenge of Public Agenda Research—1990 Presidential Address. *American Sociological Review* 56 (1): 1–14.

———. 1992. Another Look at the Truly Disadvantaged. *Political Science Quarterly* 106: 639–658.

———. 1996. *When Work Disappears: The World of the New Urban Poor.* New York: Knopf.

Witt, Robert, A. Clarke, and N. Fielding. 1999. Crime and Economic Activity: A Panel Data Approach. *British Journal of Criminology* 39 (3): 391–400.

Yinger, J. 1995. *Closed Doors, Opportunities Lost: The Continuing Costs of Housing Discrimination.* New York: Russell Sage Foundation.

Yoon, In-Jin. 1997. *On My Own: Korean Businesses and Race Relations in America.* Chicago: University of Chicago Press.

Zax, Jeffrey, and John Kain. 1996. Moving to the Suburbs: Do Relocating Companies Leave their Black Employees Behind? *Journal of Labor Economics* 52: 195–210.

Zhou, Min. 1992. *New York's Chinatown: The Socioeconomic Potential of an Urban Enclave.* Philadelphia: Temple University Press.

Index

About the Author

KAREN F. PARKER is Professor in the Department of Sociology and Criminal Justice at the University of Delaware. Her current research interests include exploring the influence of theoretical constructs associated with labor markets and structural disadvantage on urban violence, examining the contextual and spatial dynamics of policing and crime in urban communities, and incorporating change models into the study of disaggregated homicide rates at the city level. Recent publications on these topics have appeared in *Criminology*, *Social Forces*, *Social Science Quarterly*, *Social Science Research*, *Homicide Studies*, and *Crime and Delinquency*.